IS
THE BUG
DEAD
?

IS THE BUG

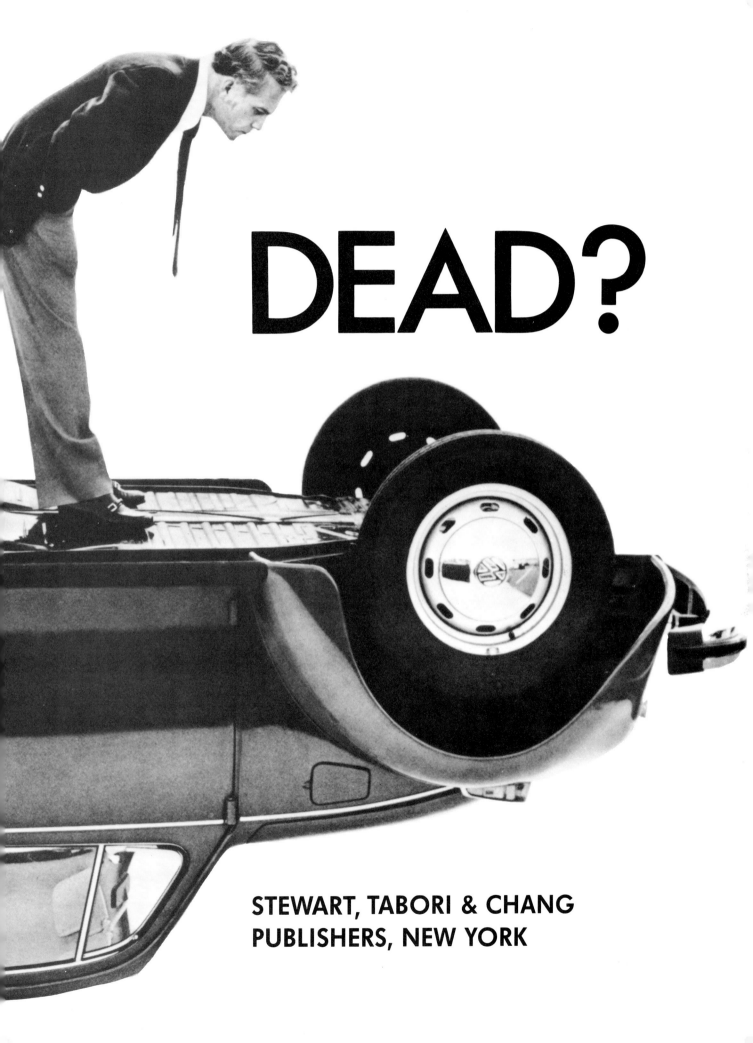

DEAD?

STEWART, TABORI & CHANG
PUBLISHERS, NEW YORK

Book design: Nai Chang

Editor: Marya Dalrymple

The advertisements have been reproduced with the permission of: Volkswagen (GB) Ltd., Volkswagenwerk A.G., and Volkswagen of America.

Library of Congress in Publication Data
Main entry under title:

Is the bug dead?

   1. Advertising—Automobiles. 2. Volkswagen automobile.
HF6161.A8I8   1983   659.1'96292222'0973   82-19202
ISBN 0-941434-24-9

Published in North America in 1983 by Stewart, Tabori & Chang, Inc. This edition has been created and designed by Stewart, Tabori & Chang, Inc.

Distributed by Workman Publishing Company, Inc.
1 West 39th Street, New York 10018

Printed in the United States.

CONTENTS

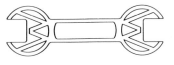

IS THE BUG DEAD?

By Alfredo Marcantonio, David Abbott, and John O'Driscoll

On the night of January 19, 1978, the unthinkable happened: Volkswagen Beetle production in Germany stopped. Owners of the 19 million Beetles that had been sold throughout the world since 1945 mourned. So did the millions of people who had *planned* to buy the little car.

The Beetle might be gone—the victim of international economics, strict EPA requirements, and changing times—but it would not readily be forgotten. Who could forget the "pregnant rollerskate," the "Love Bug," or those bumper stickers that read "Made in der Forest by der Elves"?

Who could forget the amphibious Beetles or the Formula Vee racing Beetles? Or Beetles stuffed with crazy collegians (the record was eighteen, all holding their breath in a sunroof sedan)? And what about Beetle statistics like, "The fuel used to power a Boeing 707 for an hour could drive a Beetle two and a half times around the world"? And Beetle lore: The oldest Beetle in the U.S. was built on December 30, 1945?

But most of all, who could ever forget the Beetle ads—those unconventional reminders that here was a friendly car, a car you could talk to, a car that was durable and cheap to drive, a car that would never—well, hardly ever—let you down?

Remember "Lemon." "Think Small." "Don't Laugh." "$1.02 a Pound." We couldn't let these great lines simply pass away.

Here, then, is the story of the Beetle and its legendary advertising. It is a tribute to a car that *lives*—if only in our memories.

No book about Volkswagen advertising would be complete without some reference to the Beetle's early history and some mention of the man who designed the car, Ferdinand Porsche.

Porsche, who had studied electrical engineering, turned his attention to the horseless carriage early in his career, producing a revolutionary hub-transmission system for electric cars at the age of twenty-five, in 1890. His design for this system would win him the Grand Prix at the Paris Exposition of 1900. Less than six years later, Porsche had become the director of the Austro-Daimler car company.

A string of top jobs followed for Porsche in Germany's prospering auto industry until finally, in 1931, he formed his own consulting firm, the Porsche Bureau, which specialized in automotive design. He soon emerged as probably the greatest auto engineer of his time. He was responsible for a number of ingenious designs, including the Mercedes SS sports models and the 16-cylinder, 250-mile-per-hour Auto-Union racing cars that brought Germany a clutch of Grand Prix victories in the mid-1930s.

But Porsche's dream was to produce a "people's car." Although he interested several potential manufacturers in the project, it was never developed. As it happened, the concept of a people's car was in Adolf Hitler's mind, too, and, in 1933, a meeting was arranged so that Porsche could outline his plans to the German leader. Hitler was impressed enough to offer to finance the development of the car. He insisted, however, that the car must sell for less than 1,000 marks, or about $400.

Although Porsche thought this condition was impossible, he began work in earnest. The vehicle that he set about building was unlike its contemporaries in almost every respect. The engine was cooled not by water but by air, so it would not boil or freeze. It was mounted over the back wheels to improve traction and eliminate the need for a heavy, power-absorbing drive shaft. Each wheel was sprung independently, using torsion bars instead of bulky leaf springs to save weight and space. And, most revolutionary of all, in place of a girder frame, there was a corrugated sheet-steel floor-pan chassis.

In 1937, after nearly ten years of development, the VW was ready for mass production. Hitler immediately renamed it "the Strength-through-Joy Car" or "KdF Wagen." He also instituted a special savings-stamp scheme, which would generate some of the funds needed to build a VW factory and enable the poorly paid German worker to save steadily for a car of his own.

More than 300,000 Germans saved millions of marks towards their VWs, but by the outbreak of the war not one civilian car had been produced, despite the presence of the sizable new VW factory in what would later be called Wolfsburg. Between 1939 and 1945 the Wolfsburg factory was used to produce some 50,000 VW-based Kübelwagen jeeps, Schwimmwagens (an amphibious variation), and small heating stoves for use by the troops on the Russian front.

At the end of the war, the British army took over the bombed-out plant and, scrounging for materials, managed to get production of the Beetle going for the first time. In 1945, 713 VWs rolled off the assembly line.

Three years later, anxious to capitalize on its efforts, the army offered the factory as a going concern to a number of British car makers. Ernest Breech, chairman of the Ford Motor Company, reported back to his U.S. headquarters, "Mr. Ford, I don't think what we are being offered here is worth a damn." Sir William Rootes, a member of the British Council of Motor Manufacturers, was equally unimpressed: "A car like this will remain popular for two or three years, if that. To build the car commercially would be a completely uneconomic enterprise."

The man who proved these experts wrong was Heinz Nordhoff, a Detroit-trained ex-director of GM's Opel subsidiary, whom the British army put in charge of the Wolfsburg factory early in 1948. Under his leadership, production and sales rose steadily: 6,000 cars were produced at Wolfsburg in 1947; 19,000 in 1950. In 1960, 865,000 Beetles were being turned out annually. By 1968, when Nordhoff

died, the number of VWs produced each year topped 1.6 million.

The Beetle was well on its way to a convincing takeover of the Model T Ford's title as the world's most-produced car.

The Beetle was far from unknown in the United States when the Doyle Dane Bernbach advertising agency was awarded the VW account in 1959. A steady stream of VWs had been reaching the States since the end of the Second World War, and during the mid-1950s the flow had swollen to a torrent.

In 1953, after a couple of independent attempts to import its car to the U.S., VW managed to establish a strong network of distributors and dealers. The effect on the company's sales was dramatic. Just over 2,000 VWs were sold in the States in 1953. By 1959, sales had topped 150,000.

This change of fortune is even more remarkable when you consider just how odd those early Beetles must have appeared to American eyes. At least other European imports of the day had hoods and trunks, small though they were. The Beetle was so rounded at front and rear that it was hard to tell if it was coming or going. As one wit said at the time, "It looked like a motorized tortoise."

But by the early 1950s, the Beetle had become very attractive to the growing number of U.S. drivers who were sick of the big-car diet dished up by Detroit: vast, thirsty machines that sprouted annual changes for obsolescence's sake. This disenchanted minority gave Europe's car makers their first foothold in the huge U.S. market. And with the dollar strong on the exchange, the Europeans were quick to take advantage of it.

Many of those early imports, however, weren't fully suited to operate in the States, and their engines proved unreliable on long runs and in very hot or cold weather. In contrast, the Beetle, with its simple, air-cooled engine, quickly earned a reputation for being a "tireless performer."

The Beetle's success in the mid-1950s had been achieved without advertising, but early in 1959, despite a six-month backlog on delivery of new cars, VW decided to engage an advertising agency. The man behind the decision was Carl H. Hahn, a German who was then the newly appointed head of Volkswagen of America and is today Chairman of the Board of Management for Volkswagenwerk in Germany. Hahn knew he had to move quickly. That autumn, Detroit's big three, Ford, GM, and Chrysler, would introduce their own compact cars in an attempt to compete with the growing number of foreign machines reaching the U.S.

Hahn was confident that advertising was the right move for VW because he suspected that at 150,000 cars per year, the company's sales in the U.S. were close to the maximum that could be achieved by word of mouth and dealer promotion alone. Finding a suitable advertising agency, however, was more difficult than he first thought. In fact, Hahn's search took him three months and, according to his own estimate, involved him in meeting more than 4,000 American admen. He was far from impressed by what he saw. At that time, the U.S. advertising industry was infatuated with research, think tanks, and brainstorming sessions. Print ads, commercials, and posters were tested before they ran, while they ran, and after they ran, and the findings were deeply analyzed in an attempt to make the sales message mean all things to all people. More often than not the results meant nothing to anyone—except, of course, to the agency and the client involved.

Car advertising was one of the worst offenders. According to Hahn, "We expected great things; but all we saw were presentations which showed Volkswagen ads that looked exactly like every other ad—an airline ad, a cigarette ad, a toothpaste ad. The only difference was that where the tube of toothpaste had been, they had placed a Volkswagen."

Hahn's fortuitous meeting with Doyle Dane

Bernbach came about in 1959 via a VW distributor named Arthur Stanton, who happened to be on VW of America's advertising committee. Stanton, impressed by ads that he had seen for Ohrbach's, a New York department store, had found out that DDB was behind them, and he asked the agency to do some ads for the launch of his new VW dealership, Queensboro Motors. He was pleased enough with the agency's work to give a favorable report on it to Hahn.

Doyle Dane Bernbach had been formed just ten years earlier, when Bill Bernbach and Ned Doyle left Grey Advertising to join the small agency run by their mutual friend Mac Dane. The new agency quickly earned a reputation for unusual, effective advertising by producing highly creative work for clients like Ohrbach's, El Al, Polaroid, and Levy's bakery ("You don't have to be Jewish to love Levy's").

In contrast to most of the agencies Hahn had interviewed, DDB didn't show speculative creative work for the Beetle. Rather, they simply presented the work they were doing for their existing clients. Hahn was so impressed by this unique approach and by the agency's integrity that he awarded DDB the Beetle account and a start-up budget of $800,000. VW's truck business went to Fuller & Smith & Ross, an agency that specialized in industrial advertising, but a year later that business, too, was handed over to DDB.

The first creative team at DDB to work on the VW account consisted of art director Helmut Krone and copywriter Julian Koenig. It proved to be an inspired match. Together with Bill Bernbach, these two men would create a look and tone of voice previously unheard of in car advertising.

But first they headed for Wolfsburg to roam the 270 acres of VW factory and to meet as many of the 44,000 VW employees as they could. According to Bernbach, "We spent days talking to engineers, production men, executives, workers on the assembly line. We marched side by side with the molten metal that hardened into the engine, and kept going until every part was finally in place. . . . We were immersed in the making of a Volkswagen and we knew what our theme had to be. We knew what distinguished the car. We knew what we had to tell the American public. We had seen the quality of the materials that were used. We had seen the almost incredible precautions taken to avoid mistakes. We had seen the costly system of inspection that turned back cars that would never have been turned down by the consumer. We had seen the impressive efficiency that resulted in such an unbelievably low price and such a quality product. We had seen the pride of craftsmanship in the worker that made him exceed even the highest standards set for him. Yes, this was an *honest* car. We had found our selling proposition."

The "honest" advertising that came out of that trip used realistic black-and-white photographs instead of the fanciful illustrations that were *de rigueur* in car ads at that time. No flattering airbrush work or lens distortion for the bug. No mansion or stable behind the car. No suave, debonair driver. And especially no admiring female. The copy treated the reader like an intelligent friend, not some anonymous moron, and it was self-deprecating rather than self-congratulatory. The overall impression was one of friendly straightforwardness and disarming truthfulness.

It's hard to imagine just how those first VW ads must have looked to the casual reader of a 1959 *New Yorker*. One thing is sure: they worked. No sooner had the campaign started running than advertising-industry researchers found that the ads were getting unusually high readership. Within a year or so, the campaign had become a conversation piece; discussions of favorite Beetle ads dominated cocktail-party and locker-room chatter across the country. Madison Avenue buzzed.

The acid test, whether or not the ads were *selling* cars, came when Detroit's compacts were launched. Within two years, Ford, GM, and Chrysler's hot new cars had caused imported-car sales in the U.S. to plummet from a high of 614,131 in 1960 to 339,160 in 1962. Surprisingly, VW sales were unaffected. In fact, they rose: 200,000 Beetles were sold in 1962.

Those extra sales, of course, were not solely to DDB's campaign. But it is clear that the advertising helped. Many VW dealers found that customers arrived in their showrooms with the headline of the latest Beetle ad on their lips.

Year after year, these imaginative messages would continue to give the little car its cachet. In 1968—VW's best year ever—423,000 Americans went out and bought the bug. Ten years later, production of the car in Germany was halted.

But the Beetle refuses to lie down. Today in the U.S., where more than 5 million bugs were sold, the resale value of the car often exceeds its original selling price. Used-car dealers claim that they can't keep the car in their lots. And although the Beetle is no longer advertised or promoted, the demand for it is still so great that hundreds of thousands continue to be produced in and exported from factories in such places as Mexico, Nigeria, and Brazil each year.

At last tally, more than 20 million bugs had been sold worldwide and most of those are still being driven. Thus, we can't help asking..

¿IS THE BUG DEAD?

OUR IMAGE

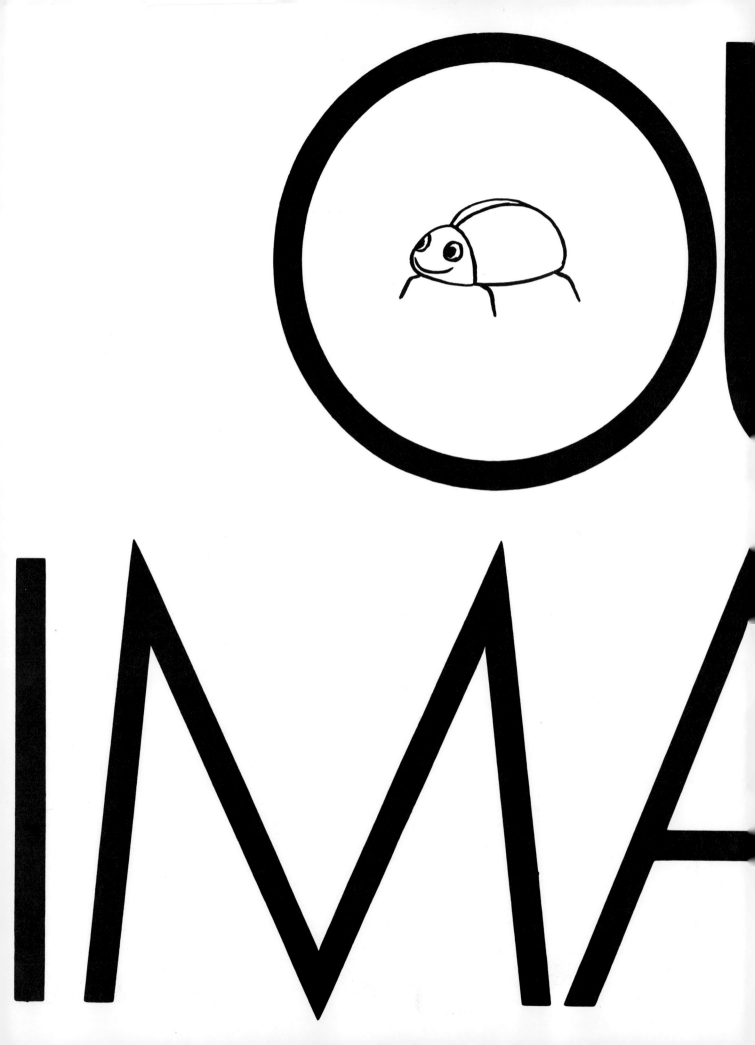

Our image.

Once upon a time, a young lady visited our plant. (In our view, the more the merrier.)

"What a sweet little car," she said. "It looks just like a beetle."

Now we're a pretty down-to-earth bunch.

At that moment we were figuring how much larger our brake-area would have to be if we stepped up our horsepower.

She stopped us cold.

After we'd made some discreet inquiries, we found out that a good many people shared her opinion.

But we also found out that people never said "beetle" nastily.

Always affectionately.

So we grew resigned to our nickname, and finally rather pleased with it.

It seems to say a lot about our attitude to car-making: determined, painstaking, unpretentious.

After all, some people try like mad to create a favorable impression.

We'd simply tried to make the Volkswagen a practical car.

And we'd gotten our very own image.

Don't let the low price scare you off.

$1574.*

That's the price of a new Volkswagen.

But some people won't buy one: They feel they deserve something costlier. That's the price we pay for the price we charge.

And some people are afraid to buy one: They don't see how we can turn out a cheap car without having it turn out cheap. This is how.

Since the factory doesn't change the bug's shape every year, we don't have to change the factory every year.

What we don't spend on looks, we spend on improvements to make more people buy the car.

Mass production cuts costs. And VWs have been produced in a greater mass (over 10 million to date) than any car model in history.

Our air-cooled rear engine cuts costs, too, by eliminating the need for a radiator, water pump, and drive shaft.

There are no fancy gadgets, run by push buttons.

(The only push buttons are on the doors. And those gadgets are run by you.)

When you buy a VW, you get what you pay for. What you don't get is frills. And you don't pay for what you don't get.

©VOLKSWAGEN OF AMERICA, INC.® SUGGESTED RETAIL PRICE, EAST COAST P.O.E., LOCAL TAXES AND OTHER DEALER DELIVERY CHARGES, IF ANY, ADDITIONAL, WHITEWALLS OPTIONAL AT EXTRA COST.

Live below your means.

If you'd like to get around the high cost of living, we have a suggestion:

Cut down on the high cost of getting around.

And buy a Volkswagen. It's only $1699*.

That's around $1200 less than the average amount paid for a new car today. (Leave it in the bank. More's coming.)

A VW saves you hundreds of dollars on upkeep over the years.

It takes pints, not quarts, of oil. Not one iota of antifreeze.

And it gets about 27 miles to the gallon. The average car (thirsty devil that it is) only gets 14.

So the more you drive, the more you save.

And chances are, you'll drive it for years and years. (Since we never change the style, a VW never goes out of style.)

Of course, a VW's not much to look at. So a lot of people buy a big flashy car just to save face.

Try putting that in the bank.

*VOLKSWAGEN OF AMERICA, INC.® SUGGESTED RETAIL PRICE, EAST COAST P.O.E. $1,777, WEST COAST P.O.E. LOCAL TAXES AND OTHER DEALER DELIVERY CHARGES, IF ANY, ADDITIONAL, WHITEWALLS OPTIONAL AT EXTRA COST.

Do you earn too much to afford one?

For many people the Volkswagen would be an ideal car. Except for one thing. It doesn't cost enough.

They're afraid nobody will know they have any money, if it doesn't show in their car. In other words, they buy their car for other people. Not themselves.

Then there are those who earn enough to buy a much better car than the VW. But they don't. Because they can't find one.

For them the best car is one that simply gets them there. Comfortably and economically. One they don't have to worry about. That doesn't make many stops for gas and rarely needs repairs.

A car where rare repairs don't cost very much. A car where the car doesn't even cost very much.

They feel they can afford to save money with a Volkswagen.

Now next time you see somebody driving a VW don't feel sorry for him.

Who knows? Someday the bank might be using his money to give you a new car loan.

With 34 wives, even a king has to cut a few corners.

Big, fast, expensive cars have always been a passion with royalty. But a family man like King Njiiri of Kenya probably doesn't have very much passion to spare.

Or very much money. (Things have been kind of slow lately in the king business.) Which makes him the kind of king that a Volkswagen is really fit for.

The price of a brand new one — $1639* —isn't much higher than the price of a brand new wife. And a VW is a lot cheaper to support.

It goes about 27 miles on a gallon of gas. About 40,000 miles on a set of tires.

A Volkswagen also comes apart very easily. (It only takes about twenty minutes to take off a fender, or 45 minutes to take out the whole engine.) That makes repairing it easy. And quite inexpensive.

But when it's not being taken apart, a VW holds together very nicely. So even though old ones cost a good deal, they're still a good deal.

Especially if you happen to get one that was owned by an elderly king who only used it to go to court.

BY APPOINTMENT TO HIS MAJESTY, KING NJIIRI

It makes your house look bigger.

Cars are getting to be bigger, so houses are getting to look smaller.

But one little Volkswagen can put everything back in its proper perspective.

A VW parked in front does big things for your house. And your garage. To say nothing of small parking spots and narrow roads.

On the other hand, a VW does make some things smaller.

Gas bills, for instance. (At 32 mpg, they'll probably be half what you pay now.)

You'll probably never add oil between changes. You'll certainly never need anti-freeze. Tires go 40,000 miles. And even insurance costs less.

One thing you'd think might be smaller in a Volkswagen is the inside.

But there's as much legroom in front of a VW as there is in the biggest cars.

When you think about it, you really have only two choices:

You can buy a bigger house for who-knows-how-much.

Or a Volkswagen for $1,595.*

Our philosophy.

We have a very simple philosophy.

It's merely a matter of questioning what people have always taken for granted.

Here's how it works:

Just because everybody else put the horsepower in front doesn't mean we had to.

(Anyone who's driven a Volkswagen in snow or mud knows where the horsepower works best. Over the drivewheels.)

Just because we sell cars doesn't put selling at the top of our agenda.

(For us, service comes first.)

Just because this is big-car country, we haven't assumed that nobody wants a small car.

(That's how the "small-car revolution" started.)

Just because most people change models, shapes, sizes, trims and so forth every year, we don't have to follow suit.

(We figure the way a car works is far more important than the way it looks.)

Back in '49, when there were just two VWs in the whole U.S.A., this way of thinking must have seemed pretty cranky.

But now?

Ugly is only skin-deep.

It may not be much to look at. But beneath that humble exterior beats an air-cooled engine. It won't boil over and ruin your piston rings. It won't freeze over and ruin your life. It's in the back of the car for better traction in snow and sand. And it will give you about 29 miles to a gallon of gas.

After a while you get to like so much about the VW, you even get to like what it looks like.

You find that there's enough legroom for almost anybody's legs. Enough headroom for almost anybody's head. With a hat on it. Snug-fitting bucket seats. Doors that close so well you can hardly close them. (They're so airtight, it's better to open the window a crack first.)

Those plain, unglamorous wheels are each suspended independently. So when a bump makes one wheel bounce, the bounce doesn't make the other wheel bump. It's things like that you pay the $1585* for, when you buy a VW. The ugliness doesn't add a thing to the cost of the car. That's the beauty of it.

It does all the work,
but on Saturday night which one goes to the party?

Once upon a time there was an ugly little bug. It could go about 27 miles on just one gallon of gas. It could go about 40,000 miles on just one set of tires. And it could park in tiny little crevices no bigger than a bug. It was just right for taking father to the train or the children to school. Or for taking mother to the grocery store, drugstore, dime store and all the other enchanting places that mothers go when everyone else is working.

The ugly little bug was just like one of the family. But alas, it wasn't beautiful.

So for any important occasion the ugly little bug would be replaced. By a big beautiful chariot, drawn by 300 horses!

Then after a time, a curious thing happened. The ugly little bug (which was made very sturdily) never got uglier. But the big beautiful chariot didn't exactly get more beautiful.

In fact, in a few years its beauty began to fade. Until, lo and behold, the ugly little bug didn't look as ugly as the big beautiful chariot!

The moral being: if you want to show you've gotten somewhere, get a big beautiful chariot. But if you simply want to get somewhere, get a bug.

20

After a few years, it starts to look beautiful.

"Ugly, isn't it?"
"No class."
"Looks like an afterthought."
"Good for laughs."
"Stubby buggy."
"El Pig-O."

New York Magazine said: "And then there is the VW, which retains its value better than anything else. A 1956 VW is worth more today than any American sedan built the same year, with the possible exception of a Cadillac."

Around 27 miles to the gallon. Pints of oil instead of quarts. No radiator. Rear engine traction. Low insurance. $1,799* is the price. Beautiful, isn't it?

LEMON

LEN

Lemon.

This Volkswagen missed the boat.

The chrome strip on the glove compartment is blemished and must be replaced. Chances are you wouldn't have noticed it; Inspector Kurt Kroner did.

There are 3,389 men at our Wolfsburg factory with only one job: to inspect Volkswagens at each stage of production. (3000 Volkswagens are produced daily; there are more inspectors than cars.)

Every shock absorber is tested (spot checking won't do), every windshield is scanned. VWs have been rejected for surface scratches barely visible to the eye.

Final inspection is really something! VW inspectors run each car off the line onto the Funktionsprüfstand (car test stand), tote up 189 check points, gun ahead to the automatic brake stand, and say "no" to one VW out of fifty.

This preoccupation with detail means the VW lasts longer and requires less maintenance, by and large, than other cars. (It also means a used VW depreciates less than any other car.)

We pluck the lemons; you get the plums.

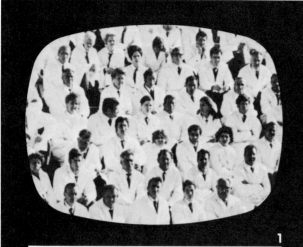

Doyle Dane Bernbach Inc.

1

Open on Roman amphitheatre filled with rows of white-coated VW inspectors.

Dramatic VO: Welcome to the Volkswagen factory, where every day a bloodthirsty mob of 8,397 inspectors decrees whether or not a Volkswagen will live. Or die.

2

Should it lose favor with any one of them . . . even for the slightest whim, it will die.

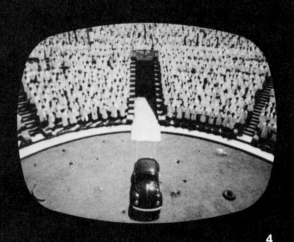

3

Should any one of its 5,000 parts be deemed defective, even for reasons unseen by the untrained eye, it will die.

4

For only after every single part has passed at least three inspections, and only after 16,000 triumphant inspections in all, may a contestant then leave this arena with the worthy title: "Volkswagen."

Now let the games begin.

SFX: Drums roll, crowd rises to its feet.

Coliseum

Every now and then a VW runs into a little trouble at the factory.

That hunk of junk was well on its way to being a Volkswagen, when it ran into a stone wall: a bunch of hard-nosed inspectors who pull enough parts off the line every day to make the equivalent of 20 cars. Or 2 freight cars full of scrap.

There are thousands of inspectors who literally pick every Volkswagen to pieces, every step of the way.

If there's a little scratch in a fender, it gets scratched. If there's a little nick in a bumper, it gets bumped.

Wherever ten people are doing something, there's an inspector to undo it. For the paint job alone, no less than 8 inspectors check every VW.

All that inspection doesn't mean the work isn't done carefully. The men who make the VW make it very well. The inspectors just make it perfect.

It takes this many men t

There are really only two things that stand between you and a new Volkswagen:

$1799.*

And 1,104 inspectors.

The money is your problem.

The number of inspectors it takes to okay each and every Volkswagen that leaves the Volkswagen factory is ours.

You see, once a man becomes a Full Inspector at our factory (and he'll spend three years doing just that), he becomes a different man.

He then has the power to overrule any and all decisions that relate to the manufacture of the car.

nspect this many Volkswagens.

(One "no" from any one of those gentlemen up in the picture and that Volkswagen is not a Volkswagen.)

Every single VW part is inspected at least 3 times. That means that before the whole car can get from us to you, it has to go through 16,000 different inspections in all.

Think of that: 16,000.

We lose an average of 225 Bugs a day that way.

So if you ever had to wait a little longer than you cared to for a new Volkswagen, now you know why:

It's not that we can't make them fast enough.

It's just that we can't make them good enough fast enough.

That's how many times we inspect a Volkswagen.

These are some of the ok's our little car has to get in our factory.

(It's easy to tell the ok's from the no's. One no is all you ever see.)

We pay 5,857 men just to look for things to say no to.

And no is no.

A visitor from Brazil once asked us what we were going to do about a roof that came through with a dent in it.

Dents are easy to hammer out.

So what we did shook him a little.

We smashed the body down to a metal lump and threw it out in the scrap pile.

We stop VWs for little things that you may never notice yourself.

The fit of the lining in the roof.

The finish in a doorjamb.

In the final inspection alone, our VW has to get through 342 points without one blackball.

One out of 50 doesn't make it. But you should see the ones that get away.

After we paint the car we paint the paint.

You should see what we do to a Volkswagen even before we paint it.

We bathe it in steam, we bathe it in alkali, we bathe it in phosphate. Then we bathe it in a neutralizing solution.

If it got any cleaner, there wouldn't be much left to paint.

Then we dunk the whole thing into a vat of slate gray primer until every square inch of metal is covered. Inside and out.

Only one domestic car maker does this. And his cars sell for 3 or 4 times as much as a Volkswagen.

(We think that the best way to make an economy car is expensively.)

After the dunking, we bake it and sand it by hand.

Then we paint it.

Then we bake it again, and sand it again by hand.

Then we paint it again.

And bake it again.

And sand it again by hand.

So after 3 times, you'd think we wouldn't bother to paint it again and bake it again. Right? Wrong.

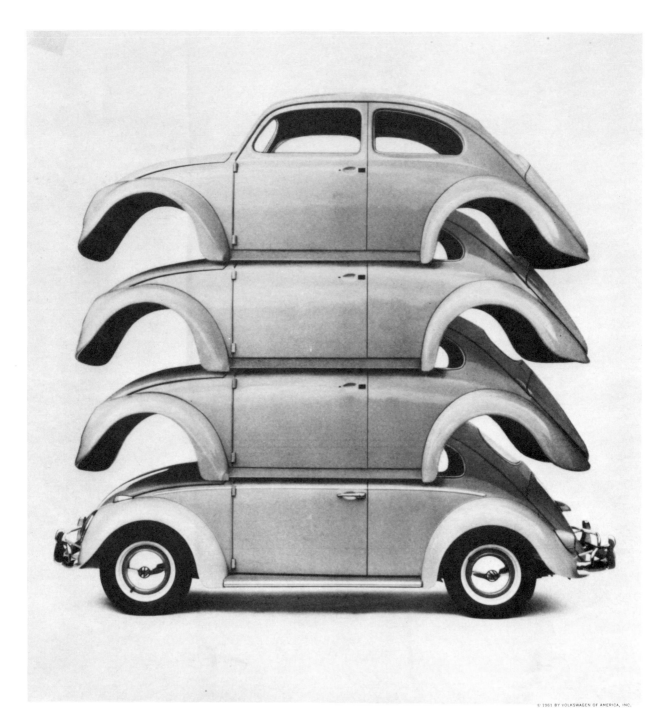

© 1961 BY VOLKSWAGEN OF AMERICA, INC.

Volkswagen overdoes it again: 4 coats of paint.

Why four coats of paint when three would be more than enough?

For the same reason that we finish the inside of the Volkswagen door jamb like the outside of the car. And seal the underside of the VW so that it's more like a ship's bottom than a car bottom.

Who'll know the difference? We will.

Let's get back to that paint job.

First the VW is literally submerged in paint; bathed in it. Then baked, and sanded. Coat No. 2 is sprayed on. Baked. Then every visible inch is sanded by hand. Coat No. 3: sprayed on. Baked. Fully sanded again. Coat No. 4: sprayed on. Baked. Whew!

Incidentally, the fourth coat is an extra

dividend the factory declared back in November. It gives the Volkswagen finish even more transparency and depth. (You don't look *at* it; you look *into* it.) And, of course, it's still another protective coat against the weather.

This is the sort of excess that makes a Volkswagen a Volkswagen.

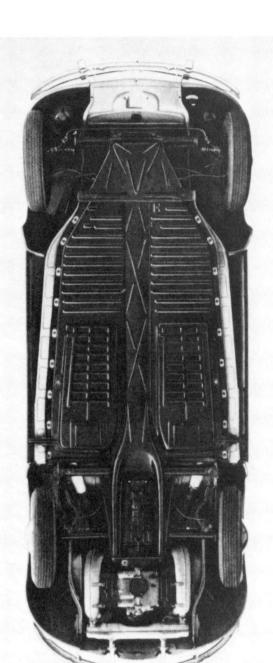

© VOLKSWAGEN OF AMERICA, INC.

Even the bottom of a Volkswagen looks funny.

We are speaking to you from underneath a Volkswagen.

Not much to look at, is there?

Too bad that big sheet of steel is in the way. Otherwise, you could see all of the Volkswagen's works.

But don't feel cheated.

That sheet of steel is the VW's bottom. No other car has anything quite like it.

It protects the VW's vital parts against everything. Including time. And it's one of the big reasons why VWs last so long.

The VW's bottom was no afterthought. It's part of the design. The car is sealed to the bottom and the bottom is sealed to the car.

Which is why a VW is practically airtight. And why some of the rumors about

floating Volkswagens aren't just rumors.

The VW's funny-looking top and funny-looking bottom have one thing in common: they both work to make the Volkswagen as good as it is.

It would be easy enough to change them.

But we think we'll leave bad enough alone.

35

1

Open on VW floating in water tank.

MVO: What makes a Volkswagen the most seaworthy car on the road?

2

A sheet of steel seals the bottom fore and aft. And the top part is practically airtight.

3

So a Volkswagen can definitely float.

4

But not indefinitely.

Floating Car

Volkswagen's unique construction keeps dampness out.

For years there have been rumors about floating Volkswagens. (The photographer claims this one stayed up for 42 minutes.) Why not?

The bottom of the Volkswagen isn't like ordinary car bottoms. A sheet of flat steel runs underneath the car, sealing the bottom fore and aft.

That's not done to make a bad boat out of it, just a better car. The sealed bottom protects a VW from water, dirt and salt. All the nasty things on the road that eventually eat up a car.

The top part of a Volkswagen is also very seaworthy. It's practically airtight. So airtight that it's hard to close the door without rolling down the window a bit.

But there's still one thing to keep in mind if you own a Volkswagen. Even if it could definitely float, it couldn't float indefinitely.

So drive around the big puddles. Especially if they're big enough to have a name.

Every new one comes slightly used.

The road to becoming a Volkswagen is a rough one. The obstacles are many.

Some make it.

Some crack.

Those who make it are scrutinized by 8,397 inspectors. (807 of whom are finicky women.)

They're subjected to 16,000 different inspections.

They're driven the equivalent of 3 miles on a special test stand.

Every engine is broken in.

Every transmission.

Many bugs are then plucked from the production line. Their sole function in life is to be tested and not to be sold:

We put them through water to make sure they don't leak.

We put them through mud and salt to make sure they won't rust.

They climb hills to test handbrakes and clutches.

Then comes the dreaded wind tunnel and a trip over 8 different road surfaces to check out the ride.

Torsion bars are twisted 100,000 times to make sure they torsion properly.

Keys are turned on 25,000 times to make sure they don't break off in keylocks.

And so it goes on.

200 Volkswagens are rejected every day.

It's a tough league.

The inside is finished like the outside.

This is our idea of a grand opening.

We took a Volkswagen apart so that you can see for yourself what the inside looks like.

You won't find one dribble on the paint or one nick on the chrome. Not one wrinkle, not one missed stitch.

VW has a bevy of seamstresses to make sure nothing zags when it should zig.

Maybe you think quality isn't something you can quite put your finger on. But just run that finger underneath the dashboard. Smooth?

Along the headliner. Smooth?

Under the door. Smooth?

Smooth.

It's one of the old VW family recipes a lot of patience plus a lot of paint.

A customer once asked, "4 coats of paint? Isn't that putting it on a bit thick?"

We said, "No."

We don't count on the paint to hold the VW together. But it keeps it from falling apart.

Think small.

Our little car isn't so much of a novelty any more.

A couple of dozen college kids don't try to squeeze inside it.

The guy at the gas station doesn't ask where the gas goes.

Nobody even stares at our shape.

In fact, some people who drive our little flivver don't even think 32 miles to the gallon is going any great guns.

Or using five pints of oil instead of five quarts.

Or never needing anti-freeze.

Or racking up 40,000 miles on a set of tires.

That's because once you get used to some of our economies, you don't even think about them any more.

Except when you squeeze into a small parking spot. Or renew your small insurance. Or pay a small repair bill. Or trade in your old VW for a new one.

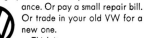

Think it over.

Doyle Dane Bernbach Inc.

1

Open on VW pulling up at the foot of a very grand building.

MVO: The Volkswagen is one of the tallest cars in the world.

2

So there's more than enough head room.

3

4

Even for the little woman.

Little Woman

They said it couldn't be done.
It couldn't.

We tried. Lord knows we tried. But no amount of pivoting or faking could squeeze the Philadelphia 76ers' Wilt Chamberlain into the front seat of a Volkswagen.

So if you're 7'1" tall like Wilt, our car is not for you.

But maybe you're a mere 6'7".

In that case, you'd be small enough to appreciate what a big thing we've made of the Volkswagen.

There's more headroom than you'd expect. (Over 37½" from seat to roof.)

And there's more legroom in front than you'd get in a limousine. Because the engine's tucked over the rear wheels where it's out of the way (and where it can give the most traction).

You can put 2 medium-sized suitcases up front (where the engine isn't), and 3 fair-sized kids in the back seat. And you can sleep an enormous infant in back of the back seat.

Actually, there's only one part of a VW that you can't put much into.

The gas tank.

But you can get about 29 miles per gallon out of it.

47

Mass production (Ford's Model T): "Any color you want, as long as it's black," was the theory. Henry Ford built one standard model that almost everyone could afford to buy. The "T" put the country on wheels.

Streamlining (Chrysler's Airflow): The Airflow was the first new car that looked like a new car. It was a magnificent flop in 1934 because it was way ahead of its time. But it left its mark on every car since.

he automotive world.

The small car (Volkswagen's Volkswagen): The VW came along and offered a sensible size, low price, high gas mileage, utter reliability, careful workmanship and a shape that was always in style. You can still get one.

This is why   **a Volkswagen has so much legroom in front.**

A Volkswagen has so much legroom in front because the engine is in back, out of the way.

How much is so much?

Believe it or not, a little VW has as much legroom as most of the biggest cars around.

As much legroom, in fact, as a limousine.

A limousine, mind you!

(And just as an aside, there's even more headroom in a VW than in a limousine.)

Frankly, we didn't put the VW engine in back just to get more legroom in front.

The original idea was to put the weight of the engine over the back wheels to get much better traction.

A Volkswagen goes where other cars won't go, even without snow tires.

So you forge ahead, with your engine behind you and your legs stretched out in front.

If you have very long legs and like to drive in the snow wearing a top hat, you might give the VW some thought.

If you wouldn't own a car in New York City, maybe you should buy a Volkswagen.

We aren't going to tell you it's fun to own a VW in New York City.

It's hard to own any kind of car here.

But a VW can take out <u>some</u> of the bumps.

Take parking. You can take leftovers. (Or if you rent garage space by the month, you can often get it for less money because a VW takes up less room.)

A VW can't get you out of a jam on the FDR Drive. But at least you won't idle away as much gas as the guy behind you. (And no matter how mad you get, you'll never boil over. Be-

cause a VW has no radiator.)

And if the bumper-to-bumper crosstown traffic gets one of your fenders, you don't have to replace half your car.

In fact, a whole brand-new VW costs only $1639, gets about 27 mpg, holds 5 pints of oil instead of 5 quarts, goes 40,000 miles on tires, and costs less for insurance and license plates.

So you not only get all the good things about owning a VW in New York.

You get all the good things about owning a VW, period.

IT STILL LOOKS THE SAME

No point showing the '62 Volkswagen. It still looks the same.

No heads will turn when you drive a '62 Volkswagen home.

(Maybe an eagle-eyed neighbor will notice that we've made the taillights a little bigger. But that's the only clue.)

We don't give car watchers much help. There are no fins on our '62 model. No new chrome. Everything is right where we left it in '61. Including the price: $0000.00.

Inside is another story.

We've put all our time and effort into improvements that matter. The '62 VW runs more quietly. New clutch and brake cables as well as steering parts never need maintenance. Heater outlets front and rear. Easier braking. And 24 more.

There's one change that's a gasser. Literally.

We've added a gas gauge. Our first.

A few die-hards may think we've stolen some of the sporting flavor from Volkswagen driving. But the gas gauge may turn out to be more useful than you'd imagine. It will not only show whether your tank is E or F; it will prove you're driving a '62.

1962 may go down in VW history as the year of the big change.

57

Practice
makes perfect.

1949

1950

1951

1952

1953

1954

1955

1956

And practice we've had plenty.

Would you believe 12 million Volkswagens all over the world? Or 3½ million here in the U.S.A.?

And, in a way, every VW we make is a little better than the one we made before.

Because we don't wrench ourselves out of shape making fake improvements every 12 months.

Instead, we make about 5,000 changes every year, that we don't even talk about. We simply do what needs doing to make the VW work better all the time. Not to look different all the time.

So what have we got to show for 25 years?

Only the most highly developed car on the road.

Take any old Volkswagen from any old year. It will still be airtight.

We never knew how to make it any other way, and we still don't. It still helps to open a window to close a door, even on an old one.

Take any new Volkswagen.

If there's a nick in the paint or on the chrome, somebody else put it there. Not us.

You won't find a jumble of wires under the dashboard. Just smooth, painted steel.

Under the hood? Shiny and smooth.

Around the engine? Shiny and smooth.

Even if you removed the door panel, you'd find it the same. Smooth and shiny.

If you saw the way we made them, you'd know why this is true.

One in eight VW employees is an inspector. And the head inspector reports to the head of the company, not to the head salesman.

Only one other car maker in the world does this; their prices start at $5,000.

Every wheel rim we turn out is inspected 100% of them. Every brake drum. Every gas tank.

Every engine is run in before it becomes part of the car. And after.

Every part that has to do with safety is individually inspected and then individually stamped with the inspector's initial.

(We also have inspectors who inspect inspectors. And until a man does it right, we don't let him put his Hans on it.)

When a VW gets to the end of the line an inspector checks to see that the engine, the electrical system, the brakes, and everything else that makes a VW stop and go puts out what we put in.

We make 5,000 cars a day; we check 5,000 cars a day.

Speaking of testing, we have 2 test tracks that are literally Hell on wheels. With hills and valleys and hairpin turns and cobblestone stretches that simply aren't found on American roads.

Every change we make (or don't make) lives or dies on one of our tracks.

By changing the way we change and testing the way we test, the Volkswagen we sell today is a whole other machine.

Over the years, we have practically doubled the VW's horsepower, but the engine should last even longer.

The luggage space in new VWs is far greater. The car is quieter and rides better. You can get a VW without a clutch pedal these days, and still get 25 miles to a gallon.

We've added thoughtful little things like a door pocket for the driver. Like tiny little

1957

1958

1959

1960

1961

1962

1963

wires that defrost the rear window electrically. Like a pop-up shield to protect the dashboard when you slide out the ashtray.

And happily, we can still sell it to you for a mere $1839.*

But when we take your $1839, we give you interest on your money by not losing interest in your car.

We are the only car people in the world with Medi-car, the Volkswagen Diagnosis System.

As part of our continuing madness, we give you 4 free top-to-bottom checkups when you buy a new VW.

You just maintain your car according to the Volkswagen maintenance schedule. If any factory part is defective in material or workmanship, any U.S. or Canadian VW dealer will repair or replace it, within 24 months or 24,000 miles, whichever comes first. And he will do it free of charge.

In short, whatever Medi-car finds that's covered by our guarantee gets fixed free.

Every last VW dealer has this electronic Medi-car equipment, and if you already own a VW, you can get the checkups for just a few dollars.

On that topic, if you do own an older Volkswagen (even a '49), and need a part, don't worry. You can drive into any VW dealer's and he won't raise an eyebrow.

He will congratulate you and fix it.

Because most VW parts, changed though they may be, still fit most VWs.

We let other people make their cars bigger and smaller and taller and shorter.

We just go on making ours longer.

1964

1965

1966

1967

1968

1969

1970

Some shapes are hard to improve on.

Ask any hen.

You just can't design a more functional shape for an egg.

And we figure the same is true of the Volks-wagen Sedan.

Don't think we haven't tried. (As a matter of fact, the VW's been changed nearly 3,000 times.)

But we can't improve our basic design.

Like the egg, it's the right kind of package for what goes inside.

So that's where most of our energy goes.

To get more power without using more gas. To put synchromesh on first gear. To improve the heater. That kind of thing.

As a result, our package carries four adults, and their luggage, at about 32 miles to a gallon of regular gas and 40,000 miles to a set of tires.

We've made a few external changes, of course. Such as push-button doorknobs.

Which is one up on the egg.

How to make a '54 look like a '64.

Paint it.

See? It looks like next year's model.

And next year's model looks like last year's model. And so it goes.

VWs always look the same because we change the car only to make it work better, never to make it look different.

So the people who bought '63 VWs aren't nervous about what the '64s will look like. And neither are we.

We've made over 5 million Volkswagens and we're still making changes.

Not enough to make you run out and buy a new one every year.

But enough to notice the differences when you do. (14 changes for '64 alone.)

In the meantime, no matter what year VW you own, you can always get parts easily; many of them are interchangeable from one year to the next.

 So if you like, you can keep your old VW running forever.

Just spray it every few years. Old paint rides again.

They don't make them like they used to.

They may still look like they used to, but that doesn't mean we still make them that way.

We used to have a tiny rear window. Now there's a big one.

We used to have a plain old rear seat. Now there's one that folds down.

Over the years, engine power has been increased by 76%.

A dual brake system has been added.

The heater is much improved.

Fact is, over the years, over 2,200 such improvements have been made. Yet, you have to be some sort of a car nut to tell a new one from an old one.

Which, of course, was the plan.

In 1949, when we decided not to out-date the bug, some of the big auto names making big, fancy changes were Kaiser, Hudson and Nash.

 Not that we were right and they were wrong, but one thing's for sure: They don't make them like they used to either.

The famous Italian designer suggested one change.

Just because the appearance of the Volkswagen doesn't change from year to year, don't think we take it for granted.

Some time ago, we called in a world-famous Italian body designer and we asked him what changes he would recommend in the design of the Volkswagen.

He studied it and studied it. Then he said, "Make the rear window larger."

"That's all?"

"That's all."

We did, starting with the '58 VW.

The Volkswagen is never changed to make it different. Only to make it better.

Changes take place throughout the year. 19 functional improvements have been made in the 1960 VW so far; improvements in handling, in ride, in durability. But your eye

wouldn't detect these changes unless we pointed them out. A nice Volkswagen touch is that most of the new parts are interchangeable; they can also be used on previous-year VWs.

 We think the Volkswagen approach to automobile design makes sense. It might even turn out to be the most advanced styling idea of all.

63

Doyle Dane Bernbach Inc.

1

Open on stand at 1940s car show.

Male Presenter: And now the star
of the 1949 Auto Show . . .
The car of the future. The car
the public wants. The all-new
De Soto.

2

Lady Presenter: Just as long
skirts will be the next look
on the fashion scene, the
Studebaker will be the next
look on the automotive scene.

3

2nd Male Presenter: There's no
doubt about it. Next year every
car in America will have holes
in its sides.

3rd Male Presenter: So the man
to see if you're buying your
next car for keeps is your
nearby Packard dealer.

Female Trio: Longer, lower,
wider, the '49 Hudson is the
car for you. . . .

4

VW Presenter: So Volkswagen will
constantly be changing, improving,
and refining this car.
Not necessarily to keep in style
with the times, but to make a
better car. Which means to all
of you . . . better mileage. . . .

MVO: Of all the promises made at
the 1949 Auto Show, we at
Volkswagen kept ours.

'49 Auto Show

How much longer can we hand you this line?

Forever, we hope.

Because we don't ever intend to change the Volkswagen's shape.

We play by our own set of rules.

The only reason we change the VW is to make it work even better.

The money we don't spend on outside changes we do spend inside the car.

This system gives us an immense advantage: Time.

We have time to improve parts and still keep most of them interchangeable.

(Which is why it's so easy to get VW parts, and why VW mechanics don't wake up screaming.)

We have time to put an immense amount of hand work into each VW, and to finish each one like a $6,000 machine.

And this system has also kept the price almost the same over the years.

Some cars keep changing and stay the same.

Volkswagens stay the same and keep changing.

69

65

Any change will be an improvement.

All we do when we change the Volkswagen is to make it work even better.
We don't play with the way it looks.
So the 1965 VW still looks the same.
And there you have the whole Volkswagen point of view:
We keep looking for ways to improve it.
And then we knock our brains out to make the new pieces fit old VWs, too.
All the improvements make a fat book.
And every one has made the car a touch better than it was before.
This year, for example, all the windows are bigger. There's more legroom in back. The heater/defroster has been improved. And so have the brakes.

Even the jack has been redesigned.
This system not only makes the VW better all the time, but also makes parts easier to get, mechanics more skillful and owners always in style.
And we can still sell it for $1,595.*
Keep the change.

The 1962½ Volkswagen.

When we find a way to improve the Volkswagen, we do it.
Then and there.
If you went out to buy a new VW today, you'd get one with an entirely new steering mechanism.
It gives you an even better sense of touch with the road and makes the VW still easier to handle.
We weren't in any rush to put it on our '62 model; it wasn't quite ready.
And we're not waiting for the '63 VW to come out; it's ready now.
We've made thousands of changes in the past 15 years. But not one has ever made a VW obsolete; only better.
People sometimes ask us why we don't change our car once a year like everybody else.
The answer is simple: once a year isn't always enough.

How can you be sure you're getting a '62?

Don't worry.
You couldn't buy a new '61 VW if you wanted to; there are none left.
Besides, there are some sure-fire ways to tell the '62 from any other year.
It just takes a little looking.
The taillights are half an inch bigger.
And the new VW also has a gas gauge.

But most of the changes can't be seen.
You feel them.
We've put new heater outlets both front and rear for more even heating.
Braking takes less pressure.
Brake, clutch and steering parts that once needed maintenance, don't any more.
Nothing on the VW can shut better.

So we've made a few things stay open better: Doorstops that work. A spring to hold the front hood open.
In all, there are 28 significant changes.
But not one of them makes last year's model obsolete.
And that's the way it'll be in '63, too.

How to tell the year of a Volkswagen.

(It isn't easy. We never change it to make it look different, only to make it work better.)

1952-1955. '52 was the last year we split the rear window. In '53, the VW sprouted front window vents. And by '55, flashing directional signals replaced those funny-looking little arms.

1956 Or is it a '57? This one's tricky. Look for twin exhausts plus an oval rear window.

1957 No visible change

1958 A famous Italian designer suggested we make the rear window bigger. We did.

1959 We changed the door handles from the pull type to the new push-button type.

1960 Look for the new medallion design on the front. (You may need your glasses.)

1961 Your clue is the windshield washer nozzle on the hood. (Standard equipment.)

1962 Bigger tail lights. (Final proof: Peek inside. Only the '62s have a gas gauge.)

66

Introducing two of the most radical changes in Volkswagen history. Can you spot them?

Did you notice that the headlights are vertical now instead of leaning back a bit? That doesn't make the car look any better. But it makes the road look better by making the lights a little brighter.

And that little hump in the back? We did that to hold the license plate up straight so the police can read it better. (Sorry.)

What you won't notice without driving the new model are the big improvements.

The engine has been enlarged to a fe-
rocious 53 horsepower. That only adds 3 m.p.h. to the top speed. Because we put most of the additional power where it would make the engine accelerate faster, turn slower and last even longer.

Now that the VW is getting to be such a hot car, we put in a couple of things to slow it down. Dual brakes.

The front wheel brakes are completely independent of the rear wheel brakes. So if you ever lost the front wheel brakes,
you could still stop the back of the car. (Which automatically stops the front too.)

The new VW also has seat belts, back-up lights and recessed door handles as standard equipment. In fact, this year we made so many changes on the VW that we thought we'd better make one more.

We wrote "Volkswagen" on the back of the car to be sure everybody would know what it was.

Never.

We'd no sooner make an over-chromed, two-tone Volkswagen than we'd change the classic beetle shape.

It's not that the chromed version looks so bad, it just doesn't make the car work any better.

That's the rule of thumb we go by: we change the VW only to improve it, not to
make last year's model look obsolete.

In 1961, for example, we were able to get more horsepower from our air-cooled engine without making it any bigger or less economical.

(One thing did get bigger this year: the tail lights.)

Everything on the VW happens for a
reason; nothing is for show.

We don't even have a chrome piece that spells out our name.

We do have a little round emblem with our initials on it, though.

After all, we can't let 600,000 Americans go riding around in unidentified cars.

We don't have to start from scratch each year.

We've been making the same basic VW for so long now, you'd think we'd be bored with the whole thing.

But the fact is, we're still learning.

We've learned how to finish the car superbly. And how to make the parts fit so well, the car is practically airtight.

So we have plenty of time to concentrate on making the car work even better.
This year the brakes are more efficient, and the heater, and some 20 other things.

When we do make new parts we try to make them fit older models, too. So there's nothing to stop a Volkswagen from running forever.

And nothing to stop it from looking new forever, either.

Starting from scratch each year can get
in the way of all that.

Just when they've ironed out the kinks in the current model, they have to face the kinks in the next.

We'll never understand all the hoopla over the "big changes" for next year's models.

Weren't they proud of this year's?

Mr. Kennedy and his 1947, 1955, 1956, 1958, 1961, 1962, 1963, 1965 Volkswagen.

As long as Michael Kennedy can remember, there's always been a bug around the house.

In all, his family has owned about 15 VWs (give or take a few aunts and uncles).

So when Mr. Kennedy decided to buy one for himself, he knew enough about it to have a little fun.
He bought the body of a '47 VW and the chassis of a '55 VW. And put them together.

Then he added a '55 engine, '55 doors, '56 seats, '58 bumpers, '61 tail lights, a '62 fender, a '63 front end and a '65 transmission. (Plus a few more odds and ends.)

The 18 years' difference between the oldest part and the newest part didn't
make any difference.

Many VW parts are interchangeable from one year to the next. (So there'll never be any part we can't replace in a hurry.)

If you'd rather not buy a VW the do-it-yourself way, don't worry.

At no extra charge, we'll do it ourselves.

67

Wha

The Jones drive a Volkswagen and V
wagens look alike from year to year.

A Volkswagen is never outmoded. In
no one knows how long a Volkswagen
the first VWs made have not worn out

ear car do the Jones drive?

from VW owners who have clocked 100,000 miles without engine repair (if ever should need it, they will find VW ce is as good as the car).

e Volkswagen *does* change — where it counts. An anti-sway bar has just been added to the front suspension to make curves even smoother. New insulation deadens engine and roadway noise.

Over the years almost every part in the Volkswagen has been changed (but not its heart or face).

 Volkswagen owners find this a happy way to drive — and to live. How about you?

Doyle Dane Bernbach Inc.

1

Open on presenter standing between two VWs.

Presenter: Folks, trade in your old Volkswagen . . .

2

. . . on a brand new one.

3

4

Is this the new one?

Trade-In

49 TUCKER

49 PACKARD

49 DE SOTO

49 STUDEBAKER

49 VOLKSWAGEN

49 HUDSON

© VOLKSWAGEN OF AMERICA, INC.

Where are they now?

Return with us now to those wondrous days of yesteryear.

It's 1949 and automobiles are getting longer, lower and wilder.

Massive bumpers are a big hit. Fins are in. And everyone's promising to "keep in style with the times."

But then, times changed.

Massive bumpers and fins went out. So did every car shown above, except the VW.

You see, back in '49, when all those other guys were worrying about how to improve the way their cars looked, we were worrying about how to improve the way ours worked.

And you know what? 2,200 improvements later, we still worry about the same thing.

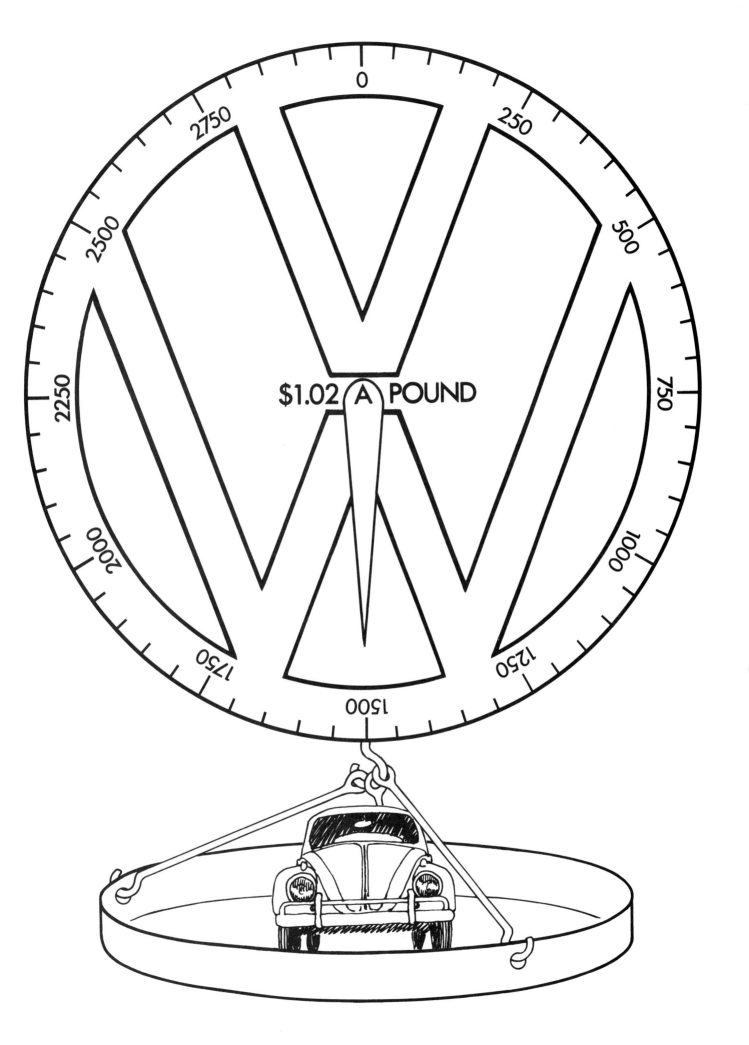

$1.02 a pound.

A new Volkswagen costs $1,595.

But that isn't as cheap as it sounds. Pound for pound, a VW costs more than practically any car you can name.

Actually, that isn't too surprising when you look into it.

Not many cars get as much put into them as a Volkswagen.

The hand work alone is striking.

VW engines are put together by hand. One by one.

And every engine is tested twice: once when it's still an engine and again when it's part of the finished car.

A Volkswagen gets painted 4 times and sanded by hand between each coat.

Even the roof lining is hand-fitted.

You won't find a nick or a dimple or a blob of glue on a VW because we aren't above rejecting a piece of car (or a whole car), if we have to.

So you can see why a Volkswagen is so expensive when you figure it by the pound.

It's something to think about.

 Particularly if you haven't bought one because you thought they didn't cost enough.

If you're not convinced the VW is an economical car, talk to some of the people who are losing a fortune on it.

Robert A. Walker
WALKER'S GULF GAS STATION
1421 Gervais Street
Columbia, South Carolina

Ronald M. Finnell
BOB'S AUTO SERVICE INC.
"Anti-freeze, tire chains and towing our specialty"
2820 South Elati Street
Englewood, Colorado

Jerry Goldfine
SAM'S AUTO REPAIRS
215 Avenue C
New York, New York

John Sheehan
JOHN SHEEHAN RECAPPING INC.
599 John Street
Bridgeport, Connecticut

Jerry T. Fuller
SUPERIOR TIRE COMPANY
530 Gervais Street
Columbia, South Carolina

Sal De Palma
DE PALMA BROTHERS
AUTO WRECKING CO.
Avenue C and Murray
Newark, New Jersey

Clyde H. Goddard
CLYDE TIRE COMPANY
12928 South Western Avenue
Gardena, California

Chuck Evan
CHUCK EVAN'S GAS & SERVICE
1600 Noblestown Rd.
Pittsburgh 5, Pa.

Robert Lagana
CHAMPION AUTO ENGINEERING
EXPERT RADIATOR REPAIRS
151 Brook Street
Eastchester, N.Y.

Don Farquhar
HOLLYWOOD TIRE COMPANY
1219 North Vine Street
Hollywood, California

Paul Tatsui
ABCO TRANSMISSION
3940 East Olympic Boulevard
Los Angeles, California

Sam Madwatkins
MATTY'S AUTO PARTS, INC.
543 West 35th Street
New York, New York

Earl C. Aeverman
DENVER ENGINE & TRANSMISSION
EXCHANGE INC.
7015 W. 36th Ave.
Wheat Ridge, Colorado

Thomas K. Cook
TOM'S AUTO SERVICENTER
977 East 21st South
Salt Lake City, Utah

There are a lot of good cars you can get for $3400. This is two of them.

If you don't happen to need two cars, there's only one thing that you need less. One car that costs as much as two cars.

Unless you want to pay a lot of money for a lot of horsepower that you'll never use. There's only one state in the country where you can go faster than a Volkswagen — Nevada. (No speed limit — they're big gamblers out there.)

The only extra horsepower you really need is for all those power gadgets. Which you need to drive a car that size. Which has to be that size to hold all those horses.

All of which also makes the average car cost almost as much to run as two Volkswagens. Considering a VW gets about 27 miles to a gallon of gas and about 40,000 miles to a set of tires.

But if you're still not sold on two bugs for the price of one beast, take advantage of this special introductory offer: one Volkswagen for half the price of two.

79

ⒸVOLKSWAGEN OF AMERICA, INC. *SUGGESTED RETAIL PRICE, EAST COAST P.O.E. ($1717 WEST COAST P.O.E.), LOCAL TAXES AND OTHER DEALER DELIVERY CHARGES, IF ANY, ADDITIONAL. WHITEWALLS OPTIONAL AT EXTRA COST.

All for the price of a fancier priced car.

$3260 is the latest average price paid for a new car these days. (So says the Automobile Manufacturers Association.)

$3260 will also buy you a new range, a new refrigerator, a new dryer, a new washer, two new television sets, a record player and a $1639* Volkswagen.

Of course our little package doesn't include all those tricky little items you find on those fancier-priced cars. (Like electric ashtray cleaners. Or headlights that disappear when the sun comes out.)

But it does include good food, clean clothes, nice music and a chance to watch all the summer reruns in color.

A lot of people frown on a Volkswagen because they feel it doesn't offer enough in the way of fancy gadgetry.

Look again.

How fancy can you get?

1

Open on funeral procession
of limousines each containing
the beneficiaries of a will.

MVO: I, Maxwell E. Snavely, being
of sound mind and body do
bequeath the following:

2

To my wife, Rose, who spent
money like there was no
tomorrow, I leave $100 and a
calendar. . . .
To my sons, Rodney and Victor,
who spent every dime I ever
gave them on fancy cars and
fast women . . .

I leave $50 in dimes. . . .

3

To my business partner, Jules,
whose motto was "Spend, spend,
spend," I leave nothing, nothing,
nothing.

And to my other friends and
relatives who also never learned
the value of a dollar, I leave . . .
a dollar.

4

Finally, to my nephew, Harold,
who ofttimes said: "A penny
saved is a penny earned." And
who also ofttimes said: "Gee,
Uncle Max, it sure pays to
own a Volkswagen. . . ."

I leave my entire fortune of
one hundred billion dollars.

Funeral

Doyle Dane Bernbach Inc.

1

Open on two identical houses.

VO: Mr. Jones and Mr. Krempler were neighbors. They each had $3,000.

2

With his money Mr. Jones bought himself a $3,000 car.

With his money Mr. Krempler bought himself . . .

3

a new refrigerator . . .
a new range . . .
a new washer . . .
a new dryer . . .
a record player . . .
two new television sets . . .
and a brand new Volkswagen.

4

Now Mr. Jones is faced with that age-old problem. . . .

Keeping up with the Kremplers.

Jones and Krempler

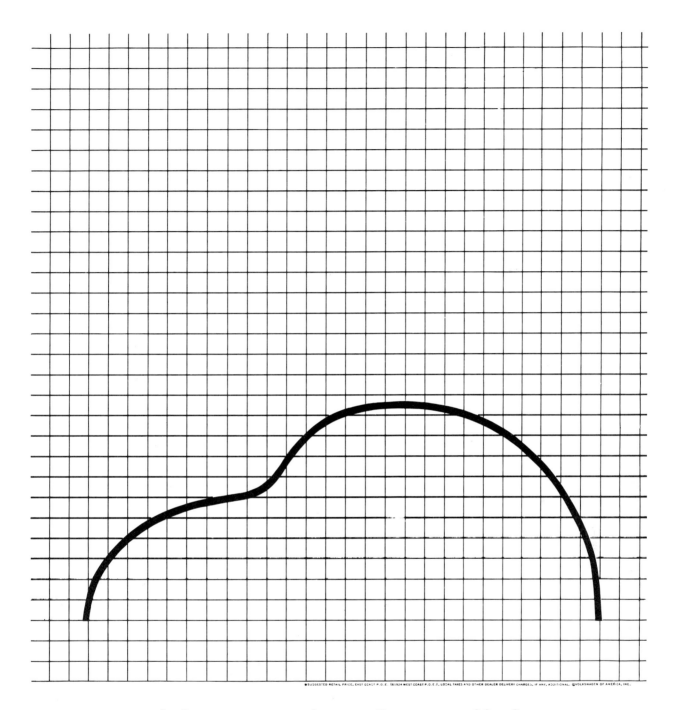

Is the economy trying to tell you something?

If you've hesitated about buying a new car because of the economy, maybe you should look into the economy of buying a new Volkswagen.

To begin with, while the average new car sells for about \$3185, a new VW sells for only \$1839*.

That saves you about \$1300.

Then, while the average car costs 10.9 cents a mile to run, a Volkswagen costs only 5 cents.

That saves you about another \$700 every year (or 12,000 miles) you drive.

And in just one year, it can bring your total savings to \$2000.

In two years, \$2700.

In three, \$3400.

Happy days are here again.

1

Open on still of VW Beetle
with price underneath.

MVO: You have exactly ten
seconds to memorize . . .

2

. . . the price of a 1971
Volkswagen Beetle.

3

4

You may take notes.

Price

The $35,000 Volkswagen.

Have we gone stark raving mad?

No, but when we heard this car was on display at the Los Angeles International Auto Show, we thought somebody had.

As it turned out, there was a method to the owner's madness.

Why not transform the world's best known economy car into the world's most economical limousine?

After all, a lot of the things that make great luxury cars great are already there in the humble little Bug:

Like 23 years of perfecting every single part of the car.

And subjecting it to over 16,000 different inspections before we sell it to you.

And having it worth lots of money to you when you sell it to someone else.

So why not stretch it out to limo length?

Why not add an intercom, bar and mahogany woodwork and tufted English upholstery and a carriage lamp to signal the doorman?

Why not be the savingest millionaire on the road?

That, children, is exactly how the rich get richer.

If gas pains persist, try Volkswagen.

©VOLKSWAGEN OF AMERICA, INC.

A VW goes a long way in relieving gas problems—by getting terrific gas mileage.

It also relieves those little headaches—by needing pints of oil instead of quarts. And <u>not</u> needing antifreeze.

Plus it gets rid of nervous upsets due to owning a new car. With Volkswagen's Owner's Security Blanket, you're provided with the best care any car can have...in sickness and in health.

The fact is Volkswagen can cure lots of problems that most cars can't.

Maybe you should take two.

Can you still get prime quality for $1.26 a pound?

A pound of Volkswagen isn't cheap compared to other cars. But what you pay for is the quality. Prime quality.

Just look at what you get for your money:

13 pounds of paint, some of it in places you can't even see. (So you can leave a Volkswagen out overnight and it won't spoil.)

A watertight, airtight, sealed steel bottom that protects against rocks, rain, rust and rot.

Over 1,000 inspections per one Beetle.

1,014 inspectors who are so finicky that they reject parts you could easily ride around with and not even detect there was anything wrong.

Electronic Diagnosis that tells you what's right and wrong with important parts of your car.

A 1600 cc aluminum-magnesium engine that gets 25* miles to a gallon of regular gasoline.

Volkswagen's traditionally high resale value.

Over 22,000 changes and improvements on a car that was well built to begin with.

What with all the care we take in building every single Volkswagen, we'd like to call it a filet mignon of a car. Only one problem. It's too tough.

Few things in life work as well as a Volkswagen.

*DIN 70030

87

A rational alternative

What's right with this picture? Well if it were true, we'd be saving 28 *billion*, 560 *million* gallons of gas every year.

How did we arrive at that figure? Since we're a nation of national averages, we know the average car uses about 735 gallons of gas a year. The Beetle, 399*. Turn the eighty-five million average cars on the road right now into Beetles, and it works out to a saving of 28,560,000,000 (give or take a few gallons).

Now we haven't figured out all the water and antifreeze that would be saved with the Beetle's air-cooled engine.

Nor can we compute the extra parking space that would be around.

to rationing gas.

Not to mention all the money people ould be able to save in a world of olkswagens.

But we know for sure that this is no pe dream. There already are police car eetles up in Ossining. And a custom built, hauffeur-driven Bug in L. A. And Volks-wagen taxis all over Honduras. And a Beetle that herds cattle in Missouri.

So with gas prices going up and ration-ing becoming a reality, the Beetle never looked so good. In fact, you might almost call it beautiful.

Few things in life
work as well as a Volkswagen.

Some of the most unusual things about a Volkswagen are things you don't usually see.

Look under the fender of a Volkswagen and you'll find something you wouldn't dream of finding: paint.

We use 13 lbs. of it on every VW. And in the most unlikely places. (If you have nothing to do sometime, remove one of our inside door panels and see what's underneath.)

Under the chassis of a Volkswagen you'll find something only a handful of cars in the world have: a sealed steel bottom. This protects all those vital things inside the car from all those vile things out there on the road. (Look under *your* car and you'll see how exposed and vulnerable everything is.)

See those four wheels sticking up in the air in the picture below? Well, you can press down on any one of them and move it without any of the others moving. What this means is when the car is right side up and one wheel hits a bump, none of the other wheels feel a thing.

Now, consider that you get all these luxury car features (and more) at an economy car price . . . with economy car gas mileage . . . the most advanced car coverage in the world (Owner's Security Blanket) . . . and almost unbelievable resale value (a '72 VW retails[†] for as much today as it did new).

You couldn't find a better buy if you stood on your head.

Still $2625*

Don't laugh.

A Volkswagen police car may seem like a funny idea to you, but it makes a lot of sense to the city of Scottsboro, Alabama.

They wanted a car that could take Police Officer H. L. Wilkerson on parking meter patrol; all day, 6 days a week, in stop-and-go traffic. Without breaking down. And without breaking the taxpayers.

So, in 1964, they bought Car S-5: a VW with a dome light, siren, and 2-way radio.

That was the year of Scottsboro's only 12" snowfall. The other police cars were in trouble up to their hubcaps. But Car S-5 was a credit to the Force. It went uphill. And downhill. And Officer Wilkerson didn't even bother to put the chains on.

Officer Wilkerson isn't supposed to go after speeders. But one day (in 1965) he chased one. And caught him. It's hard to say who was more surprised.

Car S-5 still averages 29 miles per gallon. It still doesn't use any oil between changes. And it's never had a breakdown.

 After a year and a half of continuous use, it had its clutch replaced, and its valves adjusted. That is all.

There are no real Volkswagen taxis. But there is one very good fake.

Think it over, New York, Chicago, San Francisco.

We drove our Volkswagen taxi through town on the way to get its picture taken. And did we stop traffic!

You'd think it was the first sensible thing people had ever seen. And maybe it was.

A VW is 4 feet shorter than other cabs.

So a whole fleet of them is as good as getting miles of extra streets for free.

Because they're shorter, VWs get out of the way quicker. So traffic doesn't get all balled up while some lady hunts for a 5¢ tip.

The people who'd run Volkswagens could buy a lot more cabs for their money and run each one for a lot less, too.

They wouldn't need antifreeze in winter and they could forget about boiling over in summer; the VW engine is air-cooled.

Above all, the two passengers and the driver of a VW cab would have more fun than any other three people in town.

 It may sound peculiar to you to stand on a corner and yell, "Volkswagen!"

But it sounds beautiful to us.

1

Open on snow-covered
landscape in early morning
darkness.

MVO: Have you ever wondered . . .

2

. . . how the man who drives the
snowplow drives to the
snowplow?

3

This one drives a Volkswagen.

4

So you can stop wondering.

Snowplow

We finally came up with a beautiful picture of a Volkswagen.

A Volkswagen starts looking good when everything else starts looking bad.

Let's say it's late at night and you can't sleep. It's 10 below and you forgot to put antifreeze in your car.

(A Volkswagen doesn't use antifreeze. Its engine is cooled by air.)

Let's say it's now morning: You start your car and the gas gauge reads Empty.

(Even with a gallon left, you should go approximately 27 miles in a VW.)

Let's say you notice on your way out of the driveway that every other car on your block is stuck in the snow.

(A VW goes very well in snow because the engine is in the back. It gives the rear wheels much better traction.)

Let's say you make it into town and the only parking space is half a space between a snow plow and a big, fat wall.

(A VW is small enough to fit into half a parking space.)

Let's say it's now 9:15 a.m. and the only other guy in the office is your boss.

(Now what could be more beautiful than that?)

100

A Volkswagen, obviously.

It's easy to spot a Volkswagen.

Even with enough snow on it to hide the beetle shape.

It's the one that keeps moving.

A Volkswagen will even go up icy hills when other cars won't go at all because we put the engine in the back. It gives the rear wheels much better traction.

That's half the problem.

But the engine can't just be there. It has to keep working.

So we cool the VW engine with air, not water. There's no need for anti-freeze, no chance of the block cracking. (No possibility of boiling over in summer, either.) And there's no draining. No flushing. No rust.

You can park a VW outdoors in sub-zero weather or dig it out of a snowbank; it's ready to roll as soon as you turn the key.

If you happen to live where ice and snow are no problem, don't think you can't judge the VW's extraordinary abilities.

Just try it in sand or mud.

The first car at the bottom of the world.

The Australian National Research Expedition really had no choice.

They wanted a car that "any member of the party could hop into and drive off without a moment's hesitation."

And the Volkswagen just happens to fill the bill.

The big trick is the VW's air-cooled rear engine. It has no radiator. It uses no water or antifreeze. It just goes.

(Antarctica #1 stood for days at 50° below zero and started without a tremble.)

The rear engine gave the VW so much extra traction it climbed "straight up and down the slopes." (But they cheated a little; sometimes they used chains.)

Another reason the Volkswagen went where even the dogs wouldn't go is its sealed bottom.

It took an awful beating, but that's what it's there for: To protect the works inside against the weather outside.

Things got so fierce that one man said, "Now we know what it'll be like when Hell freezes over."

So if it ever does, you know what car to buy.

102

1

2

Open on spinning wheel of car stuck in snow.

VW Owner: Hi. Need a lift?

Other Driver: Oh, thanks. I don't know what's wrong. That's a wonderful car I have back there. Did you notice?

VW Owner: Yeh.

Other Driver: It's loaded. Everything they sell. Power brakes, power steering, power windows, power seats, power radio antenna.

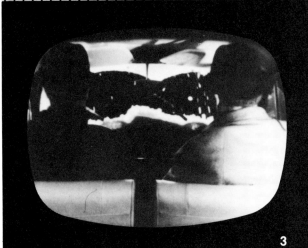

3

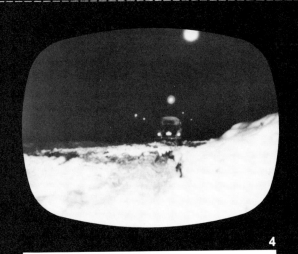

4

VW Owner: Mmm.

Other Driver: And it rides like a dream. Oh, it'll do 120 easy. 400 horses, you know. You have no idea what a sense of power that gives you. And it all works on push buttons.

Say, you're a nice guy.

VW Owner: Well, I . . .

Other Driver: Too bad you have to drive this little thing. I'm going to let you take mine for a spin. As soon as winter's over.

Spinning Wheel

Pick the right day to test drive a VW and you'll have the road to yourself.

Back when the weather was good, everybody was inviting you to come in and test drive their new whatevers.

But now that the weather isn't so good (and a test drive is really a test), the invitations have dropped off sharply.

Now maybe you can spare a little time to try out the new Volkswagen.

Not right this minute. Wait for a nice lousy day. The next time it's snowing or slushing or something like that, drive down to your VW dealer. (If you can make it in your car.)

He'll be happy to take you out and show you how a Volkswagen works when hardly anything else does.

How the weight of the motor on the rear wheels makes the VW dig in and go, in the snow or the mud, or even on ice.

As you pass all the stranded cars that passed their test drives in balmier days, he'll tell you about the VW's other cold-weather comforts.

The air-cooled motor. It doesn't freeze over, so it doesn't need anti-freeze or a winter thermostat.

And if you have to leave the car out on a cold wet night, it's got four coats of paint and a sealed bottom to keep it cozy.

 You've even got an edge with a Volkswagen if the worst happens and you get stuck.

What could be easier to push?

104

"It was the only thing to do after the mule died."

Three years back, the Hinsleys of Dora, Missouri, had a tough decision to make.

To buy a new mule.

Or invest in a used bug.

They weighed the two possibilities.

First there was the problem of the bitter Ozark winters. Tough on a warm-blooded mule. Not so tough on an air-cooled VW.

Then, what about the eating habits of the two contenders? Hay vs. gasoline.

As Mr. Hinsley puts it: "I get over eighty miles out of a dollar's worth of gas and I get where I want to go a lot quicker."

Then there's the road leading to their cabin. Many a mule pulling a wagon and many a conventional automobile has spent many an hour stuck in the mud.

As for shelter, a mule needs a barn. A

bug doesn't. "It just sets out there all day and the paint job looks near as good as the day we got it."

Finally, there was maintenance to think about. When a mule breaks down, there's only one thing to do: Shoot it.

 But if and when their bug breaks down, the Hinsleys have a Volkswagen dealer only two gallons away.

It isn't so.

That winding key you've been seeing lately on some Volkswagens is not standard equipment.

It's put there by proud VW owners, who go around telling their friends they get 40 miles on one winding.

That isn't quite true.

The correct figure is about 32 miles (regular driving), and it requires one gallon of gas.

Otherwise, the winder gives you a pretty good idea of how economical it is to keep up a VW.

The Volkswagen engine in the rear is air-cooled. No water to boil over in the summer. No water to freeze in the winter. No anti-freeze. No radiator expenses. No radiator, period.

Engine friction is so low that top speed and cruising speed are one and the same. A Volkswagen can run wide-open all day long without running up a repair bill. And it uses practically no oil between changes.

A Volkswagen costs $0,000, including heater and defroster. Leatherette upholstery is optional, and so are white wall tires, a side view mirror and radio. Outside of that, we can't think of anything else you might want.

Except possibly that winding key.

Come in today and take a turn . . . in a new VW, that is.

Impossible.

A Volkswagen can't boil over.

It's physically impossible.

The reason is absurdly simple: the VW's rear engine is cooled by air, not water.

Since air can't boil, neither can the car.

If you had to, you could drive a VW all day at top speed through a desert. Or edge along in bumper-to-bumper traffic on the hottest day of the year.

You may get all steamed up, but not your Volkswagen.

Chances are you'll appreciate the air-cooled engine even more in winter. Air can't freeze any more than it can boil. So you don't need anti-freeze. (You couldn't put any in a VW even if you wanted to; there's no radiator. And so no hoses to leak. No draining. No flushing. No rust.)

In the past, a few VW owners have been amused to find a perplexed gas station attendant with a bucket of water and no place to put it.

But we've taken care of that in our '61 model. This year, a windshield washer is standard equipment. It uses water.

Let the man fill it up.

Why so many Volkswagens live to be 100,000.

The Volkswagen isn't the kind of a car you trade in after a year or two.

It's designed and built for keeps.

The pistons in a VW travel a shorter distance per mile than almost any other car in the world. That means less wear. Engine friction and stress are so low that cruising speed is the same as top speed!

Continuity in making the same basic model year after year has led to Volkswagen's quality of assembly—the kind that a $5,000 car would be proud of; to say nothing of a car that sells for $1,565.*

Just to give you an idea: A Volkswagen is so airtight, it's a good practice to open the window before you slam the door. Even

after you've had it for several years.

So. If you own a '56 or '57 VW that you've taken good care of, why would you want to trade it in for a '61—which looks just like it?

You wouldn't.

You'd keep it, and have the pleasure of seeing 99,999 on your VW's odometer turn to xxxxx.

Can you name this car?

Clue: Even on the hottest day, you won't see this car with its hood up. (The engine is cooled by air instead of water. Won't overheat, won't freeze.)

Clue: It cruises at 70 miles an hour all day long without working up a sweat or running up a

repair bill.

Clue: In mud, sand, ice or snow, where other cars skid, this one will go. (The engine in the rear does it.)

Clue: It's put together so air-tight, there have been persistent reports it will even float.

Clue: It's never been changed for the sake of change—and it won't be, either.

Clue: It sells for $1,565,* complete with body. And a used one depreciates less than any other car.

Clue: Its initials are VW.

The only water a Volkswagen needs is the water you wash it with.

All car engines must be cooled. But how? Conventional cars are cooled by water. The Volkswagen engine is cooled by air.

The advantages are astonishing, when you think about it. Your Volkswagen cannot boil over in summer or freeze in winter, since air neither boils nor freezes.

You need no anti-freeze. You have no radiator problems. In fact, you have no radiator.

In midsummer traffic jams, your VW can idle indefinitely, while other cars and tempers boil.

The doughty Volkswagen engine is unique in still other ways. Its location in the rear means better traction (in mud, sand, ice, snow, where other cars skid, you go). And since it is cast of aluminum-magnesium alloys, you save weight and increase efficiency. Your VW delivers an honest 32 miles to the gallon, regular driving, regular gas.

And you will probably never need oil between changes.

And if you run out of gas, it's easy to push.

See?

We think of everything.

Getting a Volkswagen to the side of the road is a pushover.

It's a little surprising that VW owners don't run out of gas more often.

A figure like 32 miles to the gallon can make you a little hazy about when you last filled up.

And you spend so little time in gas stations, there are almost no reminders.

You'll probably never need oil between changes, for example.

You'll never need water or anti-freeze because the engine is air-cooled.

40,000 miles on a set of tires won't break any Volkswagen records.

And repairs are few and far between.

So this year we've installed a gas gauge to help you remember.

But we haven't taken all the fun away.

You still have to remember to look at it.

Presenting America's slowest fastback.

There are some new cars around with very streamlined roofs.

But they are not Volkswagens.

They are called fastbacks, and some of them are named after fish.

You can tell them from Volkswagens because a VW won't go over 72 mph. (Even though the speedometer shows a wildly optimistic top speed of 90.)

So you can easily break almost any speed law in the country in a VW.

And you can also cruise right past gas stations, repair shops and tire stores.

The VW engine may not be the fastest, but it's among the most advanced. It's made of magnesium alloy (one step better than aluminum). And it's so well machined you may never add oil between changes.

The VW engine is cooled by air, so it can never freeze up or boil over.

It won't have anything to do with water.

So we saw no reason to name it after a fish.

Take it for a test drive. See if you pass.

The real test in a Volkswagen is to see if you know what driving really is.

(If you think you're driving in other cars, then what you do in a Volkswagen is something else.)

Most cars give you all the lively moving sensation of sitting on your living room couch.

But the VW isn't sprung like other cars. Its 4-wheel torsion bar suspension (the kind they have in racers) gives you the feel of the road.

You always know what's going on because you know what your car's going on.

And you know what's coming, because you'll see more road than you ever saw before. (Our sloping hood doesn't cut off your view.)

When you twist the steering wheel a little, you can feel the front wheels turn a little. So you know the car's doing just what you told it to. (Doesn't that sound satisfying?)

We can tell you that the Volkswagen parks shorter than other cars, and that it maneuvers more easily.

But we can't tell you how it feels to drive one.

So take the test.

Maybe you can tell us.

After 30 Volkswagens, Father Bittman still believes.

In the beginning, Father Aloysius Bittman bought a bug.

That was in 1957 when he joined the staff of St. Anthony's Indian Mission in Mandaree, North Dakota.

Since then, Father Bittman has gone a long way. In 30 Volkswagens.

Owning two or three at a time, the Bittman staff travels 600 miles per week in each. Over dirt and gravel roads and in temperatures that have been known to go to 55 below.

A couple of Volkswagens ago, Father Bittman's '65 broke through the Garrison Reservoir ice.

"It was a good time for praying," he said.

Luckily, one 255 pound priest and one 1808 pound bug floated to safety. After the ice was chopped away and a quick oil change, the good father and his faithful companion were on their way.

He was a bit peeved about the oil change though.

"It set the Mission back $1.80," complained Father Aloysius Bittman.

33 years later, he got the bug.

We're glad that most people don't wait 33 years to buy their first Volkswagen.

But Albert Gillis did, and maybe he had the right idea all along.

He didn't buy a new car for 33 years because he didn't happen to need one.

He and his 1929 Model A Ford did just fine by each other.

He always did his own repairs and even jacked it up at night to save the tires.

When he needed a new car last year, he went out and bought a Volkswagen.

"I heard they hold up," he explained. Does he like the VW?

Mr. Gillis is 78, a Justice of the Peace, and not given to hasty decisions.

"Your inspectors sure do a good job of inspecting," was as far as he would go.

But he did mention that he and Mrs. Gillis took a trip for their 54th anniversary.

 They drove 6,750 miles and spent $62 on gas and 55¢ on oil.

"I didn't think they were supposed to burn oil," he said.

It's possible.

As far as we know, nobody has ever bought a Volkswagen because of its speed.

Its virtues have always been of the more homely kind.

An air-cooled engine that can't boil or freeze.

A paintwork job that can stay out all night and never show it.

A shape that doesn't go out of style every year, leaving the owner out of pocket.

As a result, the VW has a great image as a practical car.

And practically no image as a performance car.

And we do have a story:

The new 1500 c.c. VW does 78 mph. Fast enough to get copped for speeding on any road in the country.

In fact, in the long run, the VW can prove faster than many faster cars.

Its engine is so low-revving, it's virtually impossible to over-work it. So its top speed is also its cruising speed.

It'll go flat out, all day. From the very day you drive it out of the showroom.

Volkswagens don't need running-in.

Though the police have been known to disagree.

A rare photo.

You don't see too many pictures like this because we really never pictured ourselves this way.

For the past 23 years, while just about every other car company has been feeling the pulse of the nation and changing the looks of their cars accordingly, we've been fixing the inside of our little car just so you wouldn't have to have it fixed so often.

The result is that today, there's not one single part on a '71 Volkswagen that hasn't been improved at least once.

Recently, a top level executive from a big automotive firm summed up our position on the subject for us:

"Consumers today are more interested in quality, low cost of operation and durability, and less interested in styling, power and performance."

That's top level thinking? Our top level thinkers have been thinking that way since 1949.

September 4, 1968

Volkswagen of America
Englewood Cliffs
New Jersey

Dear Sir:

After seeing your unusual and off-beat advertisement of Volkswagens, it seems that we own one that may be of interest to you.

Below are the facts about our Volkswagen:

Purchased: ~~DePaul~~ De Paul Motors,
          Gadsden, Ala., 1961
Model: 1959
Mileage: 605,798 (only two engine changes)
Travels: Over 800 miles per day
          5 days per week.

Thank you;

Sincerely,
Mrs. Carson Brooks
210 East 4th St.
Oxford, Ala.

All good things must come to an end.

Volkswagens die. Like everything else. Only some people don't believe it.

Take Mrs. Carson Brooks of Oxford, Alabama. So far her '59 has gone over 600,000 miles. And that's with only two engine transplants.

Try telling her the end is near and she'll laugh you right off the farm.

That kind of owner loyalty begins at the VW factory where 100% of production time is spent making our little bug work better and 0% is spent making it look better (see ugly picture above).

It's the only car that's put through 15,397 inspections before it's put up for sale.

It won't give you radiator problems because we never gave it a radiator.

It comes fully equipped with 35 pounds of paint to protect its top and a protective steel bottom to protect its bottom.

So when you see one that looks on its last legs, feel no pity. It's probably led a healthier life than you have.

113

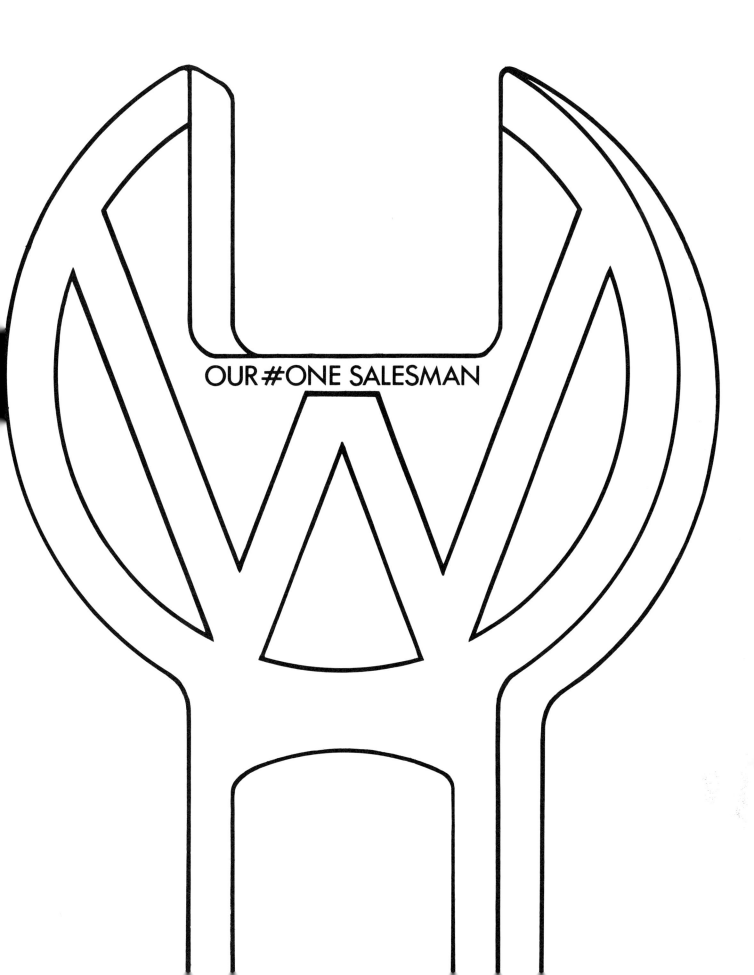

OUR #ONE SALESMAN

OUR #

SALES

Our number one salesman.

Even people who have never been near a VW can tell you how good the service is.

It's more than just a reputation.

It's become a legend.

Once you've got a legend on your hands, you've got to live up to it.

And we do.

We (and all our fellow VW dealers) see to it that you get the same front-door treatment whether you're buying a new car or having your old one greased.

It's the kind of feeling you'd hope for if you drove up in a $5,000 car.

Only you don't have to hope for it with a car that costs $0,000.00.

You get it.

Of course, the Volkswagen itself helps explain why our service is so good.

Sweeping changes are not made on the car every year; it isn't turned into a mechanic's nightmare.

Result: our mechanics have worked on the same basic car year after year. So

it's no wonder they know the car. Inside out.

And it's no wonder people who own Volkswagens keep coming back. With friends.

If that isn't a salesman, we don't know what is.

Suggestion: if you haven't got a friend who owns a VW, you can still come in yourself. And take a new VW for a drive. (When you do, you're likely to become a VW salesman, too.)

Doyle Dane Bernbach Inc.

1

Open on mechanic approaching mass of VW parts laid out on floor.

MVO: Getting out of the Volkswagen mechanic's school isn't exactly easy.

Before our mechanic works on your VW, our training instructors work on him . . .

2

. . . until he can show us where every bolt, every washer, every nut goes, what every part does, and how to service every single one of them.

3

It takes three years to make a mechanic. So no wonder there isn't anything he can't do to any Volkswagen ever made.

4

Instructor: Now, take it apart.

Student Mechanic

It takes a week to make the car. And 3 years to make the mechanic.

Oh the difference between a bug and a man.

In just seven days a piece of steel evolves into a sturdy Volkswagen.

But only after three years does a raw recruit evolve into a bona fide Volkswagen mechanic.

It's not an easy process.

He starts with a lowly doorknob and works his way up to the electrical system. (With an eagle-eyed supervisor over his shoulder.)

He takes every part apart. And puts it back together again. Over and over and over.

Then we clock him.

If he does the right job in the right time, bully for him.

He does it again.

Only after he passes the test twice do we feel he's mastered that part. And can go on to another.

But this is only part of the grind.

When this man's not working on the VW, we're working on him. At a Volkswagen training school.

There he spends seven hours a day in class studying about the car.

So by the end of his apprenticeship, he knows every nook and cranny in a VW.

For once, man counts as much as the machine.

A Volkswagen dealer is a man of many parts.

5,008 parts, to be exact.

And most of them fit any VW ever made. (Because most parts are interchangeable from one year to the next.)

Which gives the VW dealer an enormous edge.

He can repair any year Volkswagen you happen to drive up in.

All the parts are on hand or on tap.

This system also helps to explain why VW service is fast and cheap.

A fuel pump is $9.95.* A rear fender, $17.50.* Plus installation.

(And that new fender doesn't mean major surgery, either. Just 10 bolts.)

But what impresses people most about VW service is how the dealer treats them. Like a customer. Even for a 10¢ fuse.

We build the Volkswagen like a $5,000 car, so why shouldn't it get serviced like one.

Repair 'em? I've got enough parts to build 'em!

There are 5,008 parts in a Volkswagen sedan and Dale Tuttle has all of them in stock or on tap. (So does every other authorized Volkswagen dealer.)

You don't wait to get a Volkswagen serviced. Mr. Tuttle repairs even vintage VWs with equal facility; their heart and face have remained the same.

Volkswagen parts are inexpensive. A new front fender is $21.75.* A cylinder head is only $19.95.*

Volkswagen service is fast (an engine can be removed and replaced in 90 minutes.)

If you lived in Bangalore, India, and ordered a Volkswagen we wouldn't deliver it. No VW service nearby.

VW spare parts are taken from regular production, identical with those in the car itself, and so just as good.

The intriguing thing is, they are seldom needed.

Is somebody learning how to fix Volkswagens on your Volkswagen?

Anybody can put up a sign that says, "We fix Volkswagens."

But just because somebody can spell Volkswagen doesn't mean he can fix one.

VW fixing is an education unto itself.

Only there's no Volkswagen School.

There's a VW engine school.

A VW transmission school.

An electrical school. And so on and on.

The survivors of Volkswagen training schools are as much engineers as mechanics.

They know all there is to know about Volkswagens. Or else.

And so behind every genuine VW replacement part stands a calm VW dealer.

If something goes wrong—boom. Out it comes and in goes another one.

No problem.

All this is part of the quaint VW notion that the service has got to be as good as the car itself.

If it isn't, we're dead. And we know it.

So our people learn at our expense, grate on our nerves, and practice on our cars.

Not yours.

121

You don't have to replace half the car.

A new front fender for your Volkswagen doesn't mean major surgery.

Just 10 bolts, and you're in business.

We made simple maintenance a part of the Volkswagen design while the car was still on the drawing board.

And we went a lot deeper than just replacing the fenders.

A VW dealer can remove and replace the whole engine in 90 minutes.

(If you wanted to keep the engine and replace the car, it would take a little longer. But it's possible. Every part is in stock or on tap.)

Of course, the VW dealer has an edge: most parts are interchangeable from one year to the next.

So if your 1951 VW needed a fender, it wouldn't be any more trouble (or expense) than if it were a 1961.

 If you did need to replace a whole Volkswagen, they cost just $1,595* each. Brand new.

And you get to pick a new color.

122

The green fender came
    off a '58.
The blue hood came
    off a '59.
The beige fender came
    off a '64.
The turquoise door came
    off a '62.
Most VW parts
    are interchangeable
    from one year to the next.
That's why parts
    are so easy to get.

We'll fix it so good it'll be hard to close.

So it's not as depressing as it looks. Not with Volkswagen body specialists like us around.

We know all about how airtight VWs are supposed to be. So we won't be through with your door until we have to open a window to close it.

And being specialists, we can tell you better than anybody if the least expensive cure for the hammering you took is simply more hammering. Or a whole new door. (Either way, you won't take a beating. All

repairs are made at reasonable VW rates.)

If it turns out that a new door would be the best thing for you (and not just the easiest way out for us) the job's as good as finished. We stock doors to fit every model VW ever made.

And if you don't happen to drive a VW, don't let that keep us apart.

No matter what make of car you bring in for collision work, you won't leave with a bad impression.

Dealer Name

You're missing a lot when you own a Volkswagen.

A VW has fewer parts than other cars because it needs fewer parts.

It doesn't need a drive shaft to transfer engine power to the rear wheels. Because our car's engine is in back to start with (and to maintain traction with).

And it doesn't need a radiator, or a

water pump, or hoses. Because the engine's cooled with air, not water.

(When you drive your first VW, you may miss putting in antifreeze, rust inhibitors and whatnot. But you'll soon get used to it.)

The stuff a VW doesn't use, it doesn't have to haul (and waste gas on). Which

is one reason it averages 32 mpg.

And the parts you don't buy, you'll never repair. So you can't waste money on that.

Now you know why you can drive a VW for years and years with a lot of parts missing.

And never miss them.

What if you only need part of a Volkswagen?

You're in luck.

Parts of Volkswagens are easier to get than whole ones.

Any part. For any year.

That's the nice thing about making the same car year-in and year-out.

You can spend your time fiddling with the insides instead of the outside.

We've made some 3,000 improvements in our little car and hundreds of them fit our oldest models, too.

(Did you know you can get parts for a 15-year-old VW faster than for some of the new jobs around?)

Volkswagen parts are also easy to install. For instance, our fenders are bolted

on. (10 bolts do it. So you don't have to replace half the car.)

And the whole engine can be replaced in an hour and a half.

Of course, as you think about this, you may prefer to get all our new parts at once.

We have such a package.

Made in U.S.A.

George H. Long, of Grand Rapids, Mich., made this Volkswagen out of spare parts in his spare time.

The car runs very well.

But not often.

Mr. Long uses it to teach VW mechanics at one of our training schools.

They tear it to pieces and put it together

again. And again. And again.

After suffering this kind of education, our mechanics get to be pretty sharp.

(So does our service.)

Of course, we admit that our car is easier to learn about than most.

Because we don't make drastic changes every year. And because the changes we

do make, make sense.

This policy has another advantage: Since most VW parts are interchangeable from year to year, you can easily get parts for any Volkswagen.

You'll find this comforting.

If you're building your own VW.

Or buying one ready made.

"I don't want an imported car. I want a Volkswagen."

Someone actually said it.

A lady in Chicago.

She said it to one of our dealers in that city, Loop Import Motors.

Of course, the lady was mistaken; the Volkswagen *is* an imported car. But it was a revealing mistake. In those ten words, she summed up the special status of the Volkswagen in America today, and the reputation its dealers have for parts and service.

As a matter of fact, the Volkswagen dealer is as unique as the car itself.

He doesn't handle VWs as a sideline; he concentrates on this one make. But that's not all. He concentrates on one *model* that remains basically the same year after year. A tremendous advantage.

Let's take parts, for instance. Most parts for the Volkswagen are *interchangeable* from one year to the next. Even when a part is improved (and improvements take place in the VW all the time), the new part is usually designed to fit previous-year Volkswagens as well!

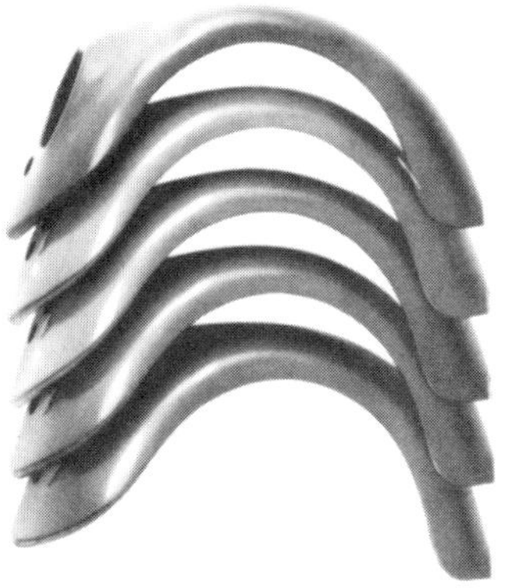

The same fender fits any year's Volkswagen.

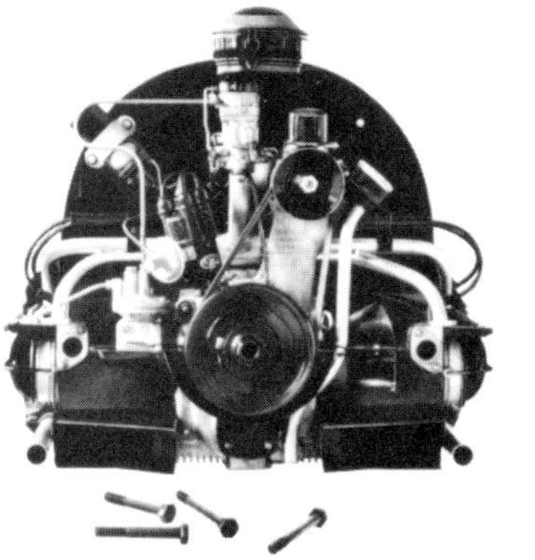

Engine can be removed and replaced in 90 minutes.

Every Authorized Volkswagen Dealer is required to stock at least $12,000 worth of parts, which would be the equivalent of a $40,000 or $50,000 parts inventory for a make that comes out with a different model every year or two. (And these are conservative figures; most VW dealers stock two or three times the minimum in parts.)

This explains why it is actually easier to get parts for a Volkswagen than for many domestic cars on the road today.

Volkswagen parts are inexpensive. A new front fender is $21.75.* A cylinder with piston and rings, $16.55.* And you'll find labor charges equally reasonable, because the Volkswagen has been deliberately designed for easy, low-cost maintenance. The car is so well conceived that the engine can be removed and replaced in only 90 minutes.

Here's another reason why VW service is so good. The Volkswagen dealer lays out his whole operation to service the one basic model. All his equipment is designed to take care of the Volkswagen; even the hoist.

The mechanics are not only factory-trained, but they've been working on this one basic model year after year, so you'd expect them to know just about everything there is to know about the car. And they do.

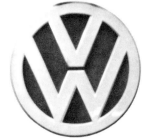

If you see this shingle, he's an authorized dealer.

There's a difference in attitude too. You feel it the first time you bring your VW back to be serviced: you get the same front-door treatment that you got when you bought the car. As a matter of fact, the newer VW dealerships don't even have a back-door or side-door entrance for service; you go in through the *front* door to deal with the service advisor.

It's the kind of an attitude you'd expect to find if you were bringing in a $6,000 car to be serviced; you get it with a car that costs only $1,565.*

The VW could never have gotten where it is today without good service. We and our dealers intend to keep it that way.

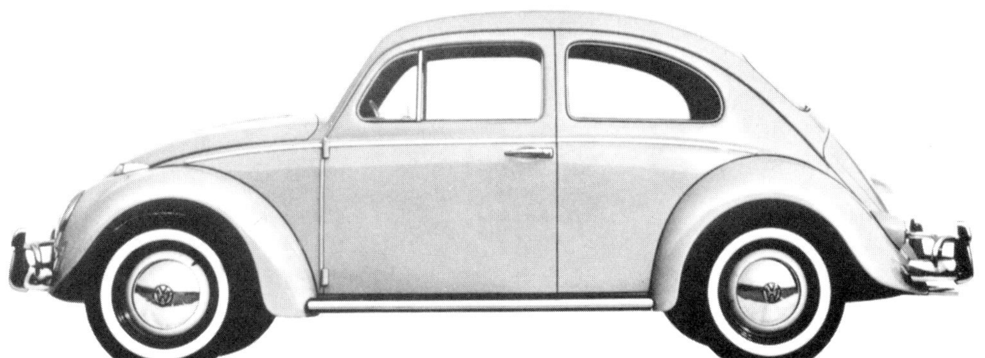

The '50, '51, '52, '53, '54, '55, '56, '57, '58, '59, '60 Volkswagen.

*SUGGESTED RETAIL PRICE, EAST COAST, P.O.E. ©1960 BY VOLKSWAGEN OF AMERICA, INC.

1

Open on announcer standing in front of curtains on stage.

Announcer: Presenting the Great Zandu.

SFX: Fanfare.

Announcer: The Great Zandu will now amaze you with his incredible mental powers.

Doyle Dane Bernbach Inc.

2

Zandu levitates VW on stage.

SFX: Oohs and ahs of the audience.

3

Car falls through floor.

MVO: When a car is essential to your job . . . you want it fixed in a hurry.

A Volkswagen dealer can replace an engine in a little over an hour. Or a fender with just ten bolts.

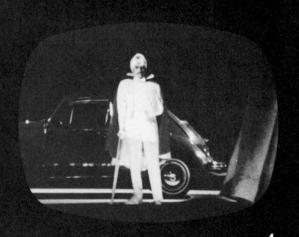

4

And with genuine Volkswagen parts always available, you'll be back to work in no time.

Announcer: Ladies and gentlemen, presenting the Great Zandu. The Great Zandu will now . . .

Cut back to curtains as they reveal fully repaired VW and partially repaired Zandu.

Zandu

Who knows what evil lurks in the hearts of used cars?

A Volkswagen dealer knows.

He knows that a used car can be a thing of beauty on the outside and a mass of corruption on the inside.

By what extraordinary power has he been able to unlock these deep, dark secrets?

By something un-mysteriously called the VW 16-point inspection.

It takes him to parts of the car rarely traveled by used car dealers... the farthest reaches of the transmission... the wilds of the electrical system... the depths of the engine.

If he finds the car to be pure at heart, he rewards it with a sign that says "The dealer guarantees 100% to repair or replace the engine, transmission, rear axle, front axle assemblies, brake system, electrical system for 30 days or 1000 miles, whichever comes first."

Good can still triumph over evil.

127

IN MEMORIAM

IN ⬗ EM

MORIAM

The Volkswagen Beetle didn't exactly take America by storm: In 1949, only two Beetles were sold in the U.S. No one wanted a small, ugly, "foreign" automobile. The rejection didn't last long. Beetle sales began to multiply so fast that in 1961 Doyle Dane Bernbach could afford to recall the bug's humble beginning.

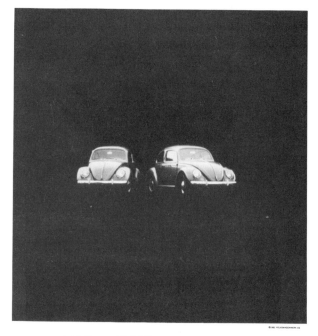

In 1949 we sold 2 Volkswagens in the U.S.A.

But the next year the Volkswagen really caught on. We sold 157.

See. You mustn't get discouraged.

It takes people a little time to get used to a new idea.

By 1960, the number of VWs in the United States had grown somewhat: 500,000.

In the last twelve months alone around 185,000 VWs were sold—including station wagons and trucks. 23% more than in '59.

But it isn't just the car they've been buying. They've been buying the VW dealer too and his counterparts all over the U.S.!

People don't buy an imported car in those numbers unless they've looked into service.

And they're not bashful, either. They stick their heads out at red lights and ask VW owners about it, point blank. They come in for a look at the parts department.

And they must like what they see and hear.

Come to think of it. It's a good thing those two lone Americans who bought VWs back in 1949 were a little more adventurous!

We've gone places!

Ten years ago, the first Volkswagens were imported into the U.S.A.

These strange little cars with their beetle shape were almost unknown.

All they had to recommend them was 32 miles to the gallon (regular gas, regular driving), an aluminum air-cooled rear engine that could go 70 mph all day long without strain, sensible size for a family, and a sensible price-tag too.

Beetles multiply; so do Volkswagens. By 1954, VW was the best-selling imported car in America. It has held that rank each year since. In 1959 over 150,000 Volkswagens were sold, including station wagons and trucks.

Millionaires buy them, so do working people and college kids. Their snub noses are familiar in every state of the Union; as American as apple strudel!

Volkswagen is an honest car. We put as much as we can into it, and we think it the best car in the world for your money. We're glad so many other people agree.

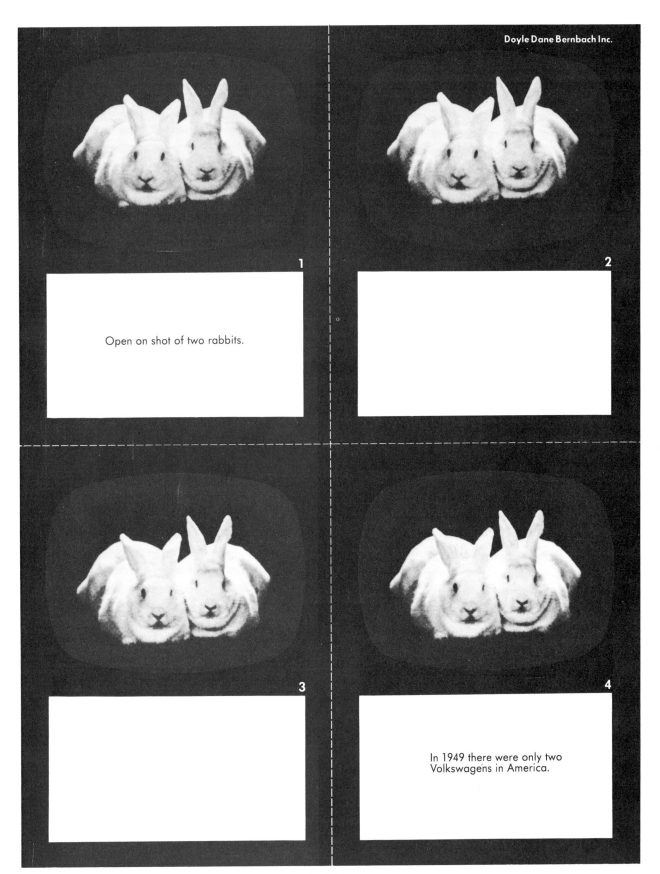

Doyle Dane Bernbach Inc.

1

Open on shot of two rabbits.

2

3

4

In 1949 there were only two
Volkswagens in America.

Rabbits

By the early 1960s, the Beetle had become as ubiquitous as Coke, and, as DDB put it, "as American as apple strudel." Hands down, it was the best-selling foreign car in America. GM, Ford, and Chrysler tried vainly to compete.

Sometimes we get the feeling we're being followed.

Everybody's getting into the act.
Everybody's making a small car.
And since we've made more of them than anyone else, we thought we'd pass along some things we've learned about the business over the years:
First off, there's no doubt about it, the only way to make an economy car is expensively.
So Rule No. 1, don't scrimp.
Get yourself the best possible engineers in the business and then hire 9,000 or so top

inspectors to keep them on their toes.
Next, try to develop an engine that's not a gas-guzzler. If you can get it to run on pints of oil instead of quarts, great. If you can get it to run on air instead of water, fantastic.
Work on things to make your car last longer. Like giving it 45 pounds of paint to protect its top and a full-length steel bottom to protect its bottom.
Important: Make sure you can service any

year car you make. There's nothing worse than having someone find out that a part they need to make their car go is no longer on hand or on tap.
Finally, spend less time worrying about what your new car looks like and more time worrying about how it works.
Perfecting a good economy car is a time-consuming business. So far it has consumed 25 years of our time.

2 shapes known   the world over.

Nobody really notices Coke bottles or Volkswagens any more.
They're so well known, they blend in with the scenery.
It doesn't matter what the scenery is, either. You can walk in and buy a VW in any one of 136 countries.
And that takes in lots of scenery.

Deserts. Mountains. Hot places. Cold places.
Volkswagens thrive.
Hot and cold don't matter; the VW engine is air-cooled.
It doesn't use water, so it can't freeze up or boil over.
And having the engine in the back makes all the difference when it comes to mud and sand and snow.

The weight is over the power wheels and so the traction is terrific.
'VWs also get along so well wherever they are because our service is as good in Tasmania as it is in Toledo.
(The only reason you can't buy a Volkswagen at the North Pole is that we won't sell you one. There's no VW

service around the corner.)
We hear that it's possible to buy yourself a Coke at the North Pole, though.
Which makes us suspect there's only one thing that can get through ahead of a Volkswagen.
A Coke truck.

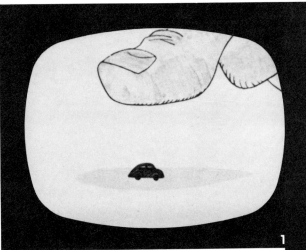

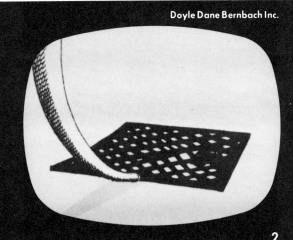

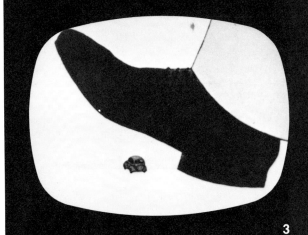

Doyle Dane Bernbach Inc.

1

Open on animated VW car "buzzing" across frame.

VO: The Beetle may look harmless to you, but a lot of people are afraid of it.

2

Ford is trying to squash it in its commercials.

Chrysler is taking swats at it too.

3

GM would like to exterminate it.

And even American Motors is doing its best to stamp it out.

4

They must be very, very jealous of the Beetle.

Why else would it bother them so much?

Fly Swatter

Doyle Dane Bernbach couldn't have known that they were predicting the future when they ran the bold headline "Will we ever kill the bug?" in 1966. In those days, VW was selling an average of 300,000 Beetles a year in America, and Detroit's compacts were just something to sniff at. Over the next few years, however, the dollar would fall drastically against the Deutsche mark, and the Environmental Protection Agency would crack down on auto safety and emission standards. These events marked the beginning of the end for the bug.

Has the Volkswagen fad died out?

Yes.
But it was an unnerving experience while it lasted.
Because after we introduced our completely sensible car, people ran out and got it for completely frivolous reasons.
The first people bought VWs just so they could be the first people to have one.
And a lady in Illinois had one because it looked cute beside her "real" car.
However, the faddists soon found out that the bug wasn't an expensive ($1,574) toy, but a cheap ($1,574*) car.
As a fad, the car was a flop:
(When you drive the latest fad to a party, and find 2 more fads ahead of you, it catches you off your avant-garde.)
But as a car, the VW was impressive:

If you had to go someplace, it took you. Even when some cars wouldn't. And when you got there, you could park it. In places where other cars couldn't.
Once people took the bug's good points for granted, it became the best-selling car model in history.
And that's when the VW fad ended.

©VOLKSWAGEN OF AMERICA, INC. *SUGGESTED RETAIL PRICE, EAST COAST P.O.E., LOCAL TAXES AND OTHER DEALER DELIVERY CHARGES, IF ANY, ADDITIONAL, WHITEWALLS OPTIONAL AT EXTRA COST.

Before you look at their new ones, look at their old ones.

Now that new car time is upon us, gosh knows, we hate to be the ones to spoil all the fun.
After all, what's more exciting than taking the family down to see the shiny new models or to hear the fast-talking salesmen, or maybe even to pick up a free balloon?
It's just that during all that hoopla and razzle-dazzle, you may not want to pick up one of those exciting new cars.
For the unpleasant fact of the matter is that junkyards throughout the country are doing a thriving business on automobiles that seemingly just yesterday were showroom stars.
Which is why we suggest a trip to the junkyard before you decide to put a new car in your own yard.
And why we suggest that that new car be a Volkswagen.
For while we can't promise you how long one will last, we can tell you that over 13 million Volkswagens are still on the road.
And when one drops out, even then it's not always destined to be dropped in a pile. For old Volkswagens have a habit of becoming other things: Like new dune buggys.
All in all, we owe it all to a decision we made 24 years ago:
To spend very little time making our little car look better. And a great deal of time making it work better.
So far, that one decision has kept us out of a lot of trouble.

Will we ever kill the bug?

Never.

How could we?

We brought the Volkswagen into the world, and gave it the best years of our life.

When people laughed at its looks, we helped it make friends all over the world. 8 million of them.

And we promised them that this was one car that would never go out of style (much less out of sight).

We won't deny that the bug's been changed. But not so you'd notice.

The 5,000-odd changes we've made since 1948 don't do a thing to the VW ex-cept make it work better and longer.

A few purists feel we kill the bug each time we improve it. But we have no choice.

We've got to keep killing the bug every chance we get.

That's the only sure way to keep it from dying.

And finally its time came. In 1977, the year U.S. Beetle sales dropped to 27,000, DDB London created the bug's swan song: "Going, going . . ." The little car that everyone thought would be around forever would no longer be exported to America.

One of the nice things about owning it is selling it.

A new Volkswagen doesn't depreciate wildly the minute you turn the key.

In a sense, the older it gets the more valuable it gets.

So that in 5 years, the same VW will be worth more than some 5-year-old cars that cost twice as much to begin with.

Old VWs are worth a lot because a lot of people want them.

One reason is that it takes a real car nut to tell a clean used one from a new one.

VWs always look like VWs.

Another reason is that they hold up.

A VW is put together so well, it's practically airtight. (It helps to open a window to close a door. Even on old ones.)

Then there's this: All the nice money you save with a new VW (on gas, oil, repairs, tires) you keep saving with an old one.

So you can get a nice price for it. (If something forces you to sell.)

It's the kind of economy that people are willing to pay an arm and a leg for.

After 3 years, the car that cost the least costs the most.

The official Used Car Guide is full of little surprises.

To show you what we mean, we've pitted one 1966 Volkswagen against 7 popular 1966 compacts.*

Back when they were spanking new, the popular compacts sold for an average price of $610 more than the Volkswagen sedan.

You'd be amazed at how unpopular they've become in 3 years.

The same compacts now sell off a used car lot for an average of $201 less than the Volkswagen.

Of course when you stop and think about it, this really isn't surprising at all.

How appealing is a car that looks 3 years old? Compared to one that never looks old?

Or a car that gets about 14 miles per gallon? Compared to one that gets about 26?

Or a car that takes lots of oil and water? Compared to one that takes little oil and no water?

The official Used Car Guide is full of foregone conclusions.

The most economical thing about a VW is how long it's economical.

This VW went 67,000 miles. And back.

Unless you've been marooned on a desert island, you probably know the Volkswagen has quite a reputation for being cheap to run.

As a matter of fact, a lot of VW owners have turned into crashing bores by talking endlessly about it.

It may be boring, but it's true.

Almost everyone gets about 29 miles to a gallon of regular gas. (Some get a bit more or a bit less depending on where and how they drive.)

It doesn't take much oil to keep a Volkswagen going. And tires that go 40,000 miles per set is no special news. (They're built to carry almost twice the weight of the car.)

The secret of more tire wear: more tire.

There aren't a lot of repairs and adjustments to put up with, either.

Parts don't cost a fortune because so many of them are interchangeable from one year to the next.

And license plates and insurance generally cost less than for other cars.

All in all, a Volkswagen can save you a good $200 a year.

Not bad.

But the thing that really sets the VW apart from other cars is its low depreciation.

The difference is staggering.

The fact is, domestic cars depreciate 2 times as fast as a Volkswagen in only one year.

A one-year-old VW that cost about $1,700* now is actually worth more than many year-old domestic cars that originally cost $2,100.

Stick around; it gets worse.

A 5-year-old Volkswagen could be sold for as much as $900 if it's in reasonably good shape.

But that 5-year-old $2,100 car is now worth maybe $400-$500. Maybe.

So it doesn't take an Einstein to figure out what an ugly hole depreciation can put in your pocket.

Unless you buy a Volkswagen.

And one Volkswagen may be the only one you'll ever have to buy.

Say you buy a 1966 VW for $1,700.*

And say you save $200 on running it every year and put it in the bank.

In 5 years or so, you can take that car (if it's in reasonable shape) together with the money you've saved to your local friendly

Volkswagen dealer.

Chances are you can drive out with a brand-new VW and not have to add a dime.

One of the nice things about owning it is selling it.

If you don't like that idea, there's another alternative.

Buy a '66 VW and just drive it.

No one will stop you from keeping the same VW for as long as you like. (No one will know the difference anyway; we never change the way it looks.)

So you can just go on saving all that nice money year after year and get rich at our expense.

Maybe the VW really can't make a poor man rich.

But neither can it make a rich man poor.

*Depending on accessories, local taxes and delivery charges.

138

Going, going...

So finally the time has come.

The Beetle is about to bid adieu.

For nearly a quarter of a century, it's been a faithful friend.

In all that time, it never set much store by the way it looked.

Only by the way it worked.

It revived the honesty of words like economical.

And reliable. And durable.

With the Beetle, you could believe them.

A lot of people did. More than 19 million altogether.

If you want to join them, you'll have to move fast.

Because the very last of the Beetles have already been brought into the country

Chin up, though.

Knowing how long Beetles last, it'll be long time before you've seen the last of them.

WHAT YEAR IS IT?

All Volkswagens were built according to calendar year prior to 1955. On August 1, 1955, a "model year" was established. In some instances, many exterior changes and inside improvements were made during a particular year's production. The older the VW, the more difficult it is to spot the changes.

The features listed are characteristic improvements in a given model year. The only sure-fire way of identification is to check the chassis number on the car and compare it with the numbers listed.

Locating Chassis Numbers

Effective with the 1970 model year, all VWs have 10-digit serial numbers in compliance with federal regulations. The first two digits of the serial number signify the model; the third is the last numeral of the model year; and the fourth to tenth digits indicate the consecutive production number within each type.

Chassis numbers are located: (1) under the back seat, stamped on the frame tunnel; (2) on the chassis identification plate; and (3) on all vehicles produced since January 1, 1969, on a vehicle identification plate fastened to the dashboard near the lower left hand corner of the windshield.

On 1965 through 1969 models, a 9-digit chassis number was used (one more digit was added where production passed one million). These numbers start with the first two digits of the model number; the third digit designates the model year. The remaining digits comprise the production numbers. All models prior to 1965 feature a 7-digit chassis number.

The 1971 and 1972 Beetles and larger Type 113 models were numbered in the same series. In 1973, the first three digits for the Beetle were 113, while the Type 113's were 133. The 1974 Beetle chassis numbers began with 114 as is the first three digits, while Type 113 started with 134. For 1975, Beetle chassis numbers were 115 2 000 001 through 115 2 267 815. For 1975 Type 113, the Beetle's chassis numbers were 135 2 000 001 through 135 2 267 815. 1975 VW Convertible series was 155 2 000 001 through 155 2 266 824. For 1976, the standard Beetle's serial numbers were 116 2 000 001 through 116 2 176 287. The VW Convertible's serial numbers for 1976 were 156 2 000 001 through 156 2 175 675. For 1977, the Beetle's serial chassis numbers were 117 2 000 001—117 2 101 292; the Convertible's were 157 2 000 001—157 2 101 292.

1949

1. License plate indentation on rear deck dropped.
2. Inside pull cable release for front hood; no lock on hood handle.
3. Solex carburetor introduced as standard equipment.
4. Starting crank hole dropped.

Chassis numbers:
91 922—138 554

1950

1. Hydraulic brakes introduced; formerly mechanical brakes.
2. Sunroof introduced.
3. Noise mufflers for heating ducts added.
4. Automatic air cooling by thermostatically controlled throttle ring.
5. Fuel mixture heating device (heat riser) introduced.

Chassis numbers:
138 555—220 471

1951

1. Chrome garnish molding added to windshield.
2. Wolfsburg crest added to front hood above hood handle.
3. Vent flaps added to front-quarter body panels.

Chassis numbers:
220 472—313 829

1952

1. Vent windows added, vent flaps in front-quarter body panels discontinued.
2. Heating control by rotary knob; formerly pull-knob.
3. "T" type rear hood handle introduced, formerly loop-type.
4. Two brake and taillights; formerly one brake and stoplight in center of rear hood.
5. Window crank makes 3½ turns; formerly 10½ turns.
6. Glove compartment gets door; formerly open bin.
7. Turn signal control moved to steering wheel from dashboard.
8. 5.60 x 15 inch tires replace 5.00 x 16 tires.
9. 2nd, 3rd and 4th gears synchronized; formerly crashbox.

Chassis numbers:
313 830—428 156

1953

1. Oval, one-piece rear window replaces split window.
2. Lock button added to vent window handles.
3. Brake fluid reservoir relocated behind spare tire; formerly at master cylinder.

Chassis numbers:
428 157—575 414

1954

1. Starter now incorporated with ignition switch; formerly separate button on dashboard.
2. Increased horsepower (from 30 to 36) and displacement (from 1131 cc to 1192 cc).
3. Oil bath air cleaner introduced; formerly felt element filter.
4. Break-in driving requirement dropped for engine.
5. Automatic three-way courtesy light added.
6. Top window in taillight housing dropped.

Chassis numbers:
575 415—722 934

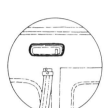

1955

1. Flashing directional indicators mounted low on front fenders to replace the semaphore turn indicators.

Chassis numbers:
722 935—929 745

1956

1. Chromed dual tail pipes added; formerly single tail pipe.
2. Taillight housing moved two inches higher.
3. Bumper overrider "bows" added.
4. Sunroof made of plastic fabric; formerly cloth.
5. Steering wheel diameter spoke (horizontal) moved lower, off-center.
6. Heater knob moved forward.
7. Adjustable front seat backs.
8. Redesigned gas tank yields larger luggage space.

Chassis numbers:
929 746—1 246 618

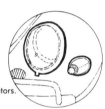

1957

1. Tubeless tires replace tube-type tires.
2. Adjustable striker plates fitted to doors.
3. Front heater outlets moved back to within five inches of door for better heat distribution.

Chassis numbers:
1 246 619—1 600 439

1958

1. Brake drums and shoes widened for faster, surer stops.
2. Rear window and windshield enlarged.
3. Front turn signal lights moved to top of fender.
4. Radio grille moved left, in front of driver.
5. Flat accelerator pedal replaces roller type.

Chassis numbers:
1 600 440—2 007 615

1959

1. Stronger clutch springs.
2. Improved fan belt.
3. Frame reinforced for greater strength.

Chassis numbers:
2 007 616—2 528 667

No Visible Changes

1960

1. Steering wheel "dished."
2. Door handles become grab-handles with pushbuttons; were formerly pull-out lever type.
3. Padded sunvisor; formerly transparent plastic.
4. Generator output increased from 160 to 180 watts.
5. Steering damper added for improved handling.
6. Seat back contoured for greater comfort.

Chassis numbers:
2 528 668—3 192 506

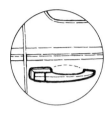

1961

1. Sunvisor and grab-handle provided for passenger's side.
2. Increased horsepower; from 36 to 40.
3. Automatic choke introduced.
4. Transmission synchronized in all forward speeds.
5. Flatter gas tank yields increased luggage space.
6. "Quick-check" transparent brake fluid reservoir.
7. Pump-type windshield washer.
8. Non-repeat starter switch.

Chassis numbers:
3 192 507—4 010 994

1962

1. Spring-loaded hood.
2. Larger taillights.
3. Sliding covers on heat outlets.
4. Compressed air windshield washer.
5. Seat belt mounting points added.
6. Gas gauge; formerly reserve fuel tap.

Chassis numbers:
4 010 995—4 846 835

1963

1. Leatherette headliner introduced.
2. Wolfsburg hood crest dropped.
3. Folding handle for sunroof.
4. Foam insulated floor.
5. Fresh air heating.
6. Nylon window guides.

Chassis numbers:
4 846 836—5 677 118

1964

1. Crank-operated sliding steel sunroof replaces the fabric sunroof.
2. Horn actuated by two thumb buttons; formerly by half-ring.
3. Larger license plate light.
4. Aerated vinyl material replaces nonporous leatherette seat upholstery.

Chassis numbers:
5 667 119—6 502 399

1965

1. Windows enlarged; slimmer door and windshield posts.
2. Heat control levers mounted on tunnel; heater efficiency improved.
3. Rear seatback converts to platform.
4. Push-button catch on engine lid.
5. Thinner, deeply contoured front seats; increased rear seat knee room.
6. Swivel mounted sunvisors.

Chassis numbers:
115 000 001—115 979 200

1966

1. Increased horsepower (from 40 to 50) and displacement (from 1200 cc to 1300 cc), number 1300 on engine lid.
2. Ventilating wheel slots; flat hub caps.
3. Emergency blinker switch.
4. Headlight dimmer switch mounted on turn signal.
5. Center-dash defroster outlet.
6. Semi-circular horn ring.

Chassis numbers:
116 000 001—116 1 021 298

1967

1. Increased horsepower (from 50 to 53) and displacement (from 1300 cc to 1500 cc).
2. Single-unit headlights with chrome rim; fender indented.
3. Dual brake system; front/rear operate independently.
4. Back-up lights.
5. Parking light incorporated into front turn signals.
6. Locking buttons on doors.
7. 12-volt electrical system (36-amp battery).
8. VOLKSWAGEN nameplate on engine lid.

Chassis numbers:
117 000 001—117 844 892

1968

1. One-piece bumpers; bows and overriders eliminated (bumper height raised).
2. Head restraints combined with front seat backrests.
3. Automatic Stick Shift (optional) introduced.
4. External gas tank filler; spring-loaded flap.
5. Front hood air intake louver; push-button front hood catch.
6. Fresh air ventilating system.
7. Collapsible steering column.
8. Exhaust emission control system.
9. Flattened door handles with built-in trigger release.
10. Back-up/brake lights and rear turn signals in single housing.
11. Certification sticker on door post that vehicle meets federal safety standards.

Chassis numbers:
118 000 000—118 1 016 098

1969

1. Rear window defogger and defroster; electric heating wires on inner surface of glass.
2. Double-jointed rear axle for improved ride and handling.
3. Warning lights in speedometer identified by letters or symbols.
4. Ignition lock is combined with a locking device for the steering wheel.
5. Gas tank filler neck flap has lock which has a release under the right side of the dash panel.
6. Front hood release is located in the glove compartment.
7. Day/night rear view mirror.
8. Warm air outlets at base of the doors moved rearward; remote control knobs on door columns.

Chassis numbers:
119 000 001—119 1 093 704

1970

1. Air intake slots on engine lid.
2. Increased horsepower (from 53 to 57) and displacement (from 1500 cc to 1600 cc).
3. Enlarged front turn signals (combined with side marker lights).
4. Reflectors mounted on rear bumper.
5. Side reflectors built into taillight housing.
6. Tenths of mile indicator on odometer (also appears on late '69 models).
7. Head restraints reduced in size.
8. Buzzer sounds when door is opened and key is left in ignition.
9. Remote control knobs for warm air outlets discontinued.
10. Lock in glove compartment door.

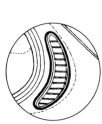

Chassis numbers:
11 0 2000001—11 0 3096945

1971

1. Increased horsepower, from 57 to 60.
2. Flow-through ventilation with exhaust ports behind rear side windows.
3. Headlights automatically go off and parking lights stay on when ignition is turned off.
4. Larger taillights.

Chassis numbers:
111 2 000001—111 3 143118

1972

1. Larger rear window.
2. Air intake slots on engine compartment increased from two to four.
3. Smoother engine warm-up after cold weather start.
4. New safety steering wheel with collapsible hub.
5. Lever mounted on steering column for fingertip control of both windshield wiper and washer.
6. Hinged parcel shelf to cover rear-end luggage well.
7. Restyled and easier-to-read speedometer.
8. Automatic electronic check of dual brake system warning light each time the engine starts.
9. VW Computer Analysis socket.

Chassis numbers:
112 2 000001—112 2 961362

1973

1. Large, circular taillight complex combining stop light, turn signal, tail and backup lights.
2. Stronger bumpers add an inch to overall length.
3. Front seats adjustable to any of 77 different positions.
4. More durable, easier-to-operate clutch; softer transmission mounting.
5. Improved intake air pre-heating for faster cold-weather starts.
6. Windshield wiper arms have black finish.
7. Inertia-reel safety belts.
8. 6.00 x 15L tires with 4½-inch-wide wheels.

Chassis numbers:
113 2 000 001—113 3 021 954

Type 113 Chassis numbers:
133 2 000 001—133 3 021 860

1974

1. Self-restoring, energy-absorbing front and rear bumpers.
2. Ignition interlock prevents engine from being started before safety belts are fastened.
3. New cylinder head alloy for better heat dissipation.
4. Additional Computer Analysis sensor reads ignition timing and top dead center.
5. Front seat headrests redesigned and made slightly smaller.
6. Steering wheel made more elastic to "give" more in the event of an accident.
7. "Park" position for Automatic Stick Shift.
8. Warning light for hand brake.

Chassis numbers:
114 2 000 001—114 2 818 456

Type 113 Chassis numbers:
134 2 000 001—134 2 798 165

1975

1. Electronic fuel injection, with "fuel injection" insignia on rear deck lid.
2. Single tailpipe.
3. Increased horsepower; 48 hp, up from 46 (SAE net).
4. Clutch pedal pressure eased.
5. Larger exhaust valve stems for better heat transfer.
6. New heat exchangers for greater heater output.
7. Installation of battery ground cable with diagnosis contact for more accurate Computer Analysis readings.
8. Odometer triggers red warning light "EGR" in speedometer to notify drivers of service requirements.
9. California models with catalytic converter require lead-free gasoline; fuel filler neck has smaller opening for nozzle.
10. Maintenance intervals extended to 15,000 miles.

Chassis numbers:
115 2 000 001—115 2 267 815

Type 113 Chassis numbers:
135 2 000 001—135 2 267 815

1976

1. Beetle has plush appearance with many luxury "extras" as standard equipment: Two-coat metallic paint (Silver Metallic, Lime Green, Topaz Metallic); full carpeting; sports-style wheel rims; rear window defogger.
2. New speedometer with outer scale in miles per hour and inner scale in kilometers per hour (on most '76 models).
3. Redesigned front seats with improved back adjustment, for added comfort and body support.
4. Two-speed fresh air blower.
5. All trim components chrome-plated.
6. Automatic stick shift (option) discontinued.

Chassis numbers:
116 2 000 001—116 2 176 287

Beetle Convertible Chassis numbers:
156 2 000 001—156 2 175 675

1977

1. Adjustable headrest replaces integrated headrest.
2. Plush velour upholstery replaces houndstooth check.
3. Electrically heated rear window (Beetle Convertible).
4. Bahama Blue Metallic paint replaces Topaz Metallic.

Beetle

Chassis numbers:
117 2 000 001—117 2 101 292

Beetle Convertible
Chassis numbers:
157 2 000 001—157 2 101 292

© Volkswagen of America, Inc.

Stewart, Tabori & Chang is indebted to Alfredo Marcantonio, David Abbott, and John O' Driscoll, whose book *Remember Those Great Volkswagen Ads?* provided the inspiration and much of the material for this book.

ACKNOWLEDGMENTS

Our thanks to the following people, without whom this book would not have seen the light of day:

Roger Baker; Donna Boland; Brian Bowler; David Brown; Tony Byrne; Martin Carey; David Cheetham; Roy Dina; Paul Garratt; Herr H. E. Hassemer; Henri Holmgren; David Horry; Graham and Emma Lincoln; John Londei; Richard Mummery; Peter Owen; Peter Pleasance; Terry Potts; John Slaven; Al Steiner; David Taylor.